The Masquerade Handbook

About the International Costumers' Guild Press

The International Costumers' Guild Press is the publication arm of the non-profit International Costumers' Guild (ICG). Its mission is to publish long-form content including books and monographs on topics related to costumes and costuming.

The ICG is an affiliation of hobbyist and professional costumers, dedicated to the promotion and education of costuming, including cosplay, as an art form in all its aspects. The ICG Press serves the ICG's mission as a non-profit educational organization.

For more information about the ICG and to locate a chapter near you, visit its website: *https://www.costume.org*.

If you have an idea for a book or a manuscript that is ready for publication, contact the Editor in Chief at *icgpress-editor@costume.org*.

International Costumers'
Guild Press

The Masquerade Handbook

The Art of Running Mid-sized Masquerade Competitions

Janet Wilson Anderson, ed.
Cat Devereaux

with Gary Anderson, Rusty Dawe,
Richard Foss, & Craig Jones

Second Edition

Produced in the United States of America.
Second Edition.
Publication Date: March 2025.
Publisher: International Costumers' Guild Press.
Cover Design: Philip Gust.
Cover Art: Michael Kelso.
(https://www.hdwallpapers.net/abstract/abstract-circles-wallpaper-585.htm)
Title Page Design: Janet Wilson Anderson.

ISBN *978-1-966384-05-2* (Softcover)
ISBN *978-1-966384-06-9* (Hardback)
ISBN *978-1-966384-07-6* (eBook)

Library of Congress Control Number: 2025933118

"We are such stuff as dreams are made on..."

Prospero, *The Tempest*

The Masquerade Handbook was originally created in 1991 and distributed in a limited edition by Janet Wilson Anderson as a compendium of articles and resources on how to run a medium-size costume competition known as a *masquerade*. It contained articles by several prominent contributors that Janet recruited to write about various aspects of running one. Janet acted as editor as well as a contributor. This work has been unavailable for over three decades.

In 2022, International Costumers' Guild Vice President Leslie L. Johnston, working with ICG members Jill Eastlake and Judy Mitchell, began a project to bring this long-out-of-print document back to life, and put it in the hands of today's costumers. Although a few things have changed (e.g. the use of cassette tapes for soundtracks), nearly all of the information in the original edition still applies today. The real value of the Handbook is gathering the collective wisdom and knowledge in one place of people with decades of experience running masquerades.

The first task was to scan the looseleaf-bound printed pages of a copy in Leslie's possession as a PDF document, and then to use optical character recognition (OCR) technology to extract as much of the text as possible. The quality of the scanned pages was not the best, which lead to errors in the OCR text that would require extensive correction.

In 2024, Leslie made her work available to the International Costumers' Guild Press to prepare a new edition for publication. After discussions with Leslie and others, the decision was made to reset the document, but to preserve the essential character of the original edition.

Kathe Gust took on the Herculean task of correcting (and in some cases reconstructing) the text generated by the OCR process. Many weeks of work resulted in a clean version of the text of the original edition. Leslie's effort to clean up scanned images was supplemented by additional work to improve the resolution for reproduction and, where necessary, to recreate them.

As an example of preserving the essence of the original edition, rules for several convention masquerades of the time that appeared in the first edition are also in this new edition. Another example is that discussions of media and audio-visual equipment then in use remain because they are still relevant and easy to apply to new types of media and equipment in use today.

No attempt was made to reorganize the contents to, for example, consolidate information covered by multiple authors. Changes were made to correct spelling, to make capitalization of terms and titles consistent, to use non-gendered pronouns, and to replace a few terms with more contemporary ones (e.g. "Den Mother" and "Mother's Helper" with "Den Leader" and "Den Helper"). Several of the authors also kindly revised their articles for clarity and to include new information, and Janet provided an introduction to this edition.

The result is a second edition of this classic work, with a new layout, typography, and graphics, that retains the essential character of the original edition that Janet and her co-authors created. I hope that you will enjoy hearing from them and learning from their experiences.

Acknowledgements

Thanks to Janet Wilson Anderson and her co-authors for creating the first edition of *The Masquerade Handbook*, and for their encouragement and kind permission to publish this second edition. Thanks also to Leslie L. Johnston, Jill Eastlake, and Judy Mitchell for initiating and laying the groundwork for this project, and for entrusting the International Costumers' Guild Press to publish it. Finally, thanks to Kathe Gust for her invaluable assistance and support in preparing this second edition.

Philip Gust,
Editor in Chief,
International Costumers' Guild Press.

I've been recalling how the whole project came into being. As I recall, Cat Devereaux was running backstage for me on the numerous masquerades I was running around the time. We were giggling at one organization meeting when she pulled out a thick folder of notes she had on backstage organization. I hauled out an equally thick folder on rules, forms, entry forms, budgets, and an article on being a judge and an early draft award titles list.

After the giggles died down, we realized that we had the nucleus of what I started calling "The Masquerade Handbook." We decided to turn it into a complete guide to running a mid-sized masquerade. We didn't include the challenges of upscaling to a Worldcon show, since there was only one of those a year, and there were dozens of cons all over the country trying to stage masquerades with no guide. Big chunks of it we knew and could put down on paper, but we realized that there were several areas that needed to be included that neither of us had the technical expertise to write.

Somehow, I ended up recruiting the additional contributors we needed and had my own in-house techno-wizard review the technical sections. And since I knew everyone and owned a large professional collating photocopier, all the pieces ended up at my house. Cat added the idea of the appendix of lists and signs, and forms, and that section kept growing. Then I put everything into sections and subsections and created the contents list. Cat and I polished our sections, added even more lists, and recruited Rick Foss to add a section on being an MC. Then I produced the section dividers, we looked through it all, and I put together the draft cover.

And then, the night before copying was due to start, I woke up in the middle of the night saying, "something is missing!!!" So, in the middle of the night, the Handbook got its overview in the form of a detailed planning timeline. This involved redoing the contents page, all the section dividers, and several other housekeeping changes. I ended up with a vastly greater appreciation of book production getting this done.

Thinking about all the work that so many people did to get *The Masquerade Handbook* out, I truly think it deserves to live again. So, on behalf of all of us, thank you for resurrecting *The Masquerade Handbook*!!!

Janet Wilson Anderson
Editor, *The Masquerade Handbook*, First Edition

TABLE OF CONTENTS

Authors: JWA: Janet Wilson Anderson, CD: Cat Devereaux, RF: Richard Foss, GA: Gary Anderson, RD: Rusty Dawe, CJ: Craig Jones.

Page numbers correspond to fixed-format versions.

Why This Handbook?

This handbook was developed to help those wonderful people who volunteer to run science fiction and fantasy masquerade competitions. The art of competitive costuming has blossomed in the last decade and the complexity associated with the masquerade has also grown. The costuming community has learned a great deal about how to stage such an event, and this handbook is the result of that often-painful learning curve. The combined experience in these pages is the outcome of dozens of such events, postmortems, discussion sessions, and personal experiences. By putting it on paper, we hope to provide a resource so the next person doesn't have to start from scratch.

What Type of Masquerade Does This Handbook Cover?

This handbook is designed for the mid-sized masquerade of approximately 15-45 entries, which takes place in conjunction with a local or regional science fiction convention. The giant competitions of Worldcon or Costume-Con have different requirements. The small local competitions can be run with somewhat less (see the "Bare Bones" section for some help with these). But the majority of masquerade competitions across the country fall in this range. The handbook assumes on-site registration, stage set-up in the late afternoon of the event, and an evening competition. If your event is different, adjust the advice and timing accordingly.

What This Handbook is Not

This handbook is not the Ultimate Rulebook, and definitely not The Only Way Things Can Be Done. This is a guidebook, full of things that have been proven to work. (Even the authors have different equally good ways of handling some things, and you will note these as you go through it.) But since the art of the masquerade keeps changing, and we keep learning new and better ways ourselves, we expect this will be updated in the future. Nothing in it is cast in stone. If you invent a better method for any aspect of this, write us, so we can include it in the next edition.

Who Are We?

The authors, Janet Wilson Anderson, Gary Anderson, Rusty Dawe, Cat Devereaux, Richard Foss and Craig Jones have been involved in masquerades for over 20 years. They have run them, competed in them, crewed them, MC'd them, judged them, teched them, and cleaned up afterwards. They gratefully admit that this is not the product of their own efforts solely, but acknowledge the contribution of vast hordes of people who have shared their knowledge and experiences with us. Special thanks go to Jeff Berry, Byron and Tina Connell, Marjii Ellers, John Fong, Marty Gear, Peggy Kennedy - editor of the *Kennedy Compendium*, Carl Mami, Lori Meltzer, Janet Moe, Drew Sanders, Karen Turner, and Kelly Turner for all we have learned from you.

Happy Masquerading!

Organization, Timetable & Check List, The Masquerade Director

-- Section 1 --

Bold = duties described in some detail.

<u>Masquerade Director</u>
    |____ <u>Director's Assistant / Gofer</u>
    |____ **<u>Operations Manager</u>**
    | |____ **<u>Lighting Head</u>**
    | | |____ <u>Lighting Crew</u>
    | |____ **<u>Audio Head</u>**
    | | |____ <u>Audio Crew</u>
    | |____ **<u>Video Head</u>**
    | | |____ <u>Video Crew</u>
    | |____ **<u>Front of House Manager</u>**
    | | |____ <u>Traffic Control & Security</u>
    | | |____ **<u>Ballroom Check-in</u>**
    | |____ **<u>Head Catcher</u>**
    | | |____ **<u>Catcher Crew</u>**
    | |____ <u>General Photo Head</u>
    | |____ <u>Photo Crew</u>
    |
    |____ **<u>Backstage Manager</u>**
    | |____ **<u>Assistant Manager</u>**
    | |____ **<u>Den Leaders</u>**
    | | |____ **<u>Den Helpers</u>**
    | |____ <u>Repair Table</u>
    | |____ **<u>Check-in</u>**
    | |____ <u>Official Photo & **Judging Photo**</u>
    | | |____ **<u>Photo Crew</u>**
    | |____ <u>Sergeant at Arms / **Head Pusher**</u>
    | |____ **<u>Pusher Crew</u>**
    |
    |____ **<u>Master of Ceremonies</u>**
    |____ **<u>Judges & Judges' Clerk(s)</u>**
    |____ <u>Calligraphy Crew</u>

Dates assume a local or regional convention and allow for comfortable planning schedules. See job descriptions for who is responsible for each of these tasks.

* Samples or write-ups given for these steps

Before Progress Report Two for the convention, or at least six months out:

Recruit Operations Manager and Backstage Manager.

Operations Manager recruits light, video and sound tech heads.

Visit venue with OM and BM and tech heads if possible.

Map ballroom, door & ceiling heights, electrical outlets, type of power supply, riser availability main corridors, service halls, bathrooms, video hook-ups.*

Do hall and stage layout.*

Write rules.*

Write tech info for contestants.*

Determine masquerade start time, crew call and contestant call. Tell appropriate Concom so rooms are available.

Find out what tech capabilities you will have.

Publish rules, layout, and tech info in PR.

Send layouts to venue liaison, con chair, and con ops.

Preliminary budget to con treasurer.

Start encouraging costumers to compete.

Four months out

Have meeting with key staff heads for full briefing on what to expect and what their needs are.

Backstage Manager recruits den staff, repair person.

Ops Manager recruits Front of House Manager.

Masquerade Director or Ops Manager recruits Photo Head.

Recruit MC.*

Determine intermission entertainment.

Get entry forms made.*

Get award certificates designed* and ribbons ordered.

Continue to recruit entries.

Two months out

Make equipment list for tech*, ops*, backstage*, photo.

Send job descriptions to key crew along with timetable, layouts, tech info, call times.*

Make supplies list.*

Continue recruiting crew.

Continue recruiting contestants.

One month out

Reconfirm with venue and venue liaison about room arrangements.

Identify rental sources and costs for tech and pipe and drape.

Recruit judges.* Send copies of rules, judges' guidelines, call times.*

Recruit secondary tech crews.

Advise convention Volunteer Coordinator of needs for security, traffic and other volunteers.

Give Concom final budget.

One week out

Assemble repair kit.*

Buy all supplies.

Start packing supplies by area.*

Confirm equipment rental arrangements.

Reconfirm venue arrangements.

Pick up ribbons; get award certificates copied.

Get all forms assembled.

Make backstage signs.*

Put together registration signs, forms, including photo sign up and supply kit.*

Reconfirm judges.

Day before Masquerade

Pick up all rental equipment.

Move all supplies & equipment to venue.

Recruit supplemental staff for helpers, walkers, catchers, pushers*.

Check rooms and Concom one last time for changes, especially time changes.

Make preliminary work schedule.*

Make security badges.*

Open registration for masquerade and photo sign-up.*

Get list from Concom of seating for VIP's.

Six hours before start time

Close registration.*

Put masquerade in order*; make running order*; number every- thing.

Number media and put them in order.*

Make many copies of running order.

List all missing signatures, media, text etc. for check-in.*

Four hours before masquerade start

Give tech forms and media to Operations Manager.*

MC forms to MC if they want them early.

Discuss running order with Backstage Manager. Determine number of dens needed and break list accordingly. Assign Den Leaders.*

Make 3 x 5 cards for check-in.

Check all supplies.

MASQUERADE DIRECTOR AND KEY CREW GO EAT!!!!

Three hours to start

Assemble all tech supplies and equipment.

Crew call for tech and front of house.*

Set up lights, sound, video.*

Tape stage*; set-up pipe and drape.

Rope off special seating.* Tell House Manager who will be where.

Post signs on entrance doors.*

Set up judges' deliberation room.*

Two hours to start

Backstage crew call.*

Set up backstage* with chairs, tables, signs.

Get water - lots of water.

Brief crew on traffic pattern, photo, seating, etc.*

Set up check-in.*

Set up judging photo area.*

Set up official photo area.

Set up general photo area.

Give photo sign-up sheets to ballroom check-in and general photo head.

Set up repair and munchies tables*.

Set up den areas backstage.*

Set up workmanship judging area.*

Set up judges' table* and get water.

Check MC podium light and put out water, flashlight.*

One- and one-half hours to start

Start contestants check in.*

Lighting, sound, video final check out.

Contestants allowed on stage to rehearse, if not before.*

Workmanship judges call.*

One hour to start

MC call to discuss entries with contestants.*

Judges' clerk's call, give judges forms, award certificates and judges' table equipment. Brief on location of judges' deliberation room.*

Check that all stage and equipment set-up is done.

One half hour to start

Judges call; judges briefed on masquerade entries, rules, scoring and introduction procedure and who is sitting where. Certificates signed.*

Ribbons and trophies located near podium.

Confirm all contestants checked in and judging photos taken. Note any changes to order for tech, judges, MC.*

MC given final list of announcements, and any changes to order.*

Judges' clerk collects judging photos.*

Check traffic paths to both entrances for obstructions.

15 minutes to start

Contestants all off stage; given 15-minute warning.*

Final backstage announcements, reminder of traffic flow, any stage problems.*

House lights on full.

All catchers, pushers and aisle people in place.*

Special seating doors open, then open for general seating.

Five minutes to start

Give five-minute warning.*

Check MC has judges' intros in right order and all announcements.*

Judges' clerk at table with judging photos, certificates, judges' forms and documentation.*

All tech staff in place. Backstage liaison on headset, ready to call masquerade for tech.*

First den of contestants lined up near staging area.

Head Pusher with final running order at main entrance.

Masquerade start

Lights down in house, Director at podium to introduce MC.

MC makes announcements, introduces judges who go sit at table.*

"Entry number One...." and we're off.

At end of run-through

Judges leave for deliberation.

Judges' clerk takes forms, judging photos, documentation, etc. *

During deliberation, clerk makes two copies of winners list.*

Contestants finish general photo. Reminded to stick around for awards.

Intermission announcements.

Intermission entertainment.

Backstage - preliminary clean up and return of property to contestants.

Judges return

Contestants assembled backstage. Told traffic flow for awards. Reminded when and where certificates will be available.

Pushers, catchers and aisle walkers back at post.*

Director collects certificates and one copy of winners list for calligraphy.

Awards announced.* Ribbons and trophies handed out.

All crew in place till final award handed out.

Director thanks crew, contestants, judges, MC and audience

After awards

Strike equipment.

Clean up backstage.

Collect all lost property.

Collect all judges and MC forms.*

Collect judging photos, documentation and media for return at post- mortem. Also Lost and Found.

Thank all crew personally.

Before post-mortem

Calligraph certificates.

Debrief key crew and ask them to attend post-mortem.

Post-convention

Return all rented equipment.

Assemble all bills to submit to treasurer.

Inventory repair kit for next time.

Write thank-you's to crew.

Publish winners list as appropriate.

Mail to winners who didn't pick up their certificates.

COLLAPSE AFTER A JOB WELL DONE.

The Masquerade Director ...

Is GHOD! The Masquerade Director is the final authority and has total responsibility! Sets policy.

Is the interface with the con committee.

Handles the budget.

Writes the Progress Report information.

Determines the masquerade rules and registration requirements. Handles all decisions relating to these as well as pre-con correspondence.

Selects Backstage Manager, Operations Manager, judges, and MC (and anyone else they want to). On politically heavy cons, this should include the judges' clerk. Decides the halftime entertainment.

Determines the running order of contestants and of the MC's presentation including anything remotely related to the awards.

Grants any exceptions to the rules as they see fit.

Gives the heads of tech and backstage multiple copies of the running order as soon as possible.

Works with the heads of tech, house and backstage to coordinate things within their areas (but lets them relay the information to their areas in an orderly manner). In return, Masquerade Director should expect the department heads to keep them informed of any special problems while fighting the small fires themselves.

Handles all political decisions. (Safety issues in presentations; if a contestant will still be allowed to show their costume in a masquerade even if they are ineligible to compete; if a person should be removed from backstage if creating too big of a problem; if a person should be allowed to compete or be dropped at the last minute; etc.)

During the show the Masquerade Director should be able to depend on the crew heads to take care of almost all emergencies. Actual job position is... any place she/he wishes to be. Normal spots, depending on what crew is in place, may be checking the final line-up just before the contestants go on or just acting as an interface with tech to the stage area. A bored Masquerade Director has a good crew.

At half-time, the Masquerade Director worries over the judges.

Does or delegates anything and everything they wish to.

The division of duties between a Masquerade Director and Backstage Manager is always at the Masquerade Director's discretion. The less experienced· the Backstage Manager, the more the Masquerade Director should monitor, help recruit the crew and handle the marginal duties.

At local cons, the Backstage Manager often is only the caretaker for the backstage area during the masquerade. For large cons, the two should start working together before the masquerade weekend even if that action is only a few phone calls to determine the budget, equipment requirements and the work split. There is nothing wrong with sharing knowledge and expertise.

Stage Layout,
Rules,
Contestant Info

-- Section 2 --

MAIN HALL AND STAGE LAYOUT CONSIDERATIONS

by Janet Wilson Anderson

The layout you select for the masquerade staging, traffic flow and seating will be largely determined by the venue (hotel or other facility) you are in. If you have options, the following come into consideration:

1. Is the main hall big enough for the audience, technical equipment, stage, wings, judges seating and at least one wide-width exit aisle? Your stage size may be limited by the amount of space available after everything else that has to go in the hall is accounted for.

2. Is there a way to handle two-sided entrances? Many presentations need to enter from both sides and providing for this will often determine just where in the hall the stage is set up. Remember, some venues can be persuaded to let you go through the service hallways, but these will have to be checked just before the show for obstacles (wet floors, room service carts, glass racks etc.)

3. Where can you put the green room for easy access to the hall? Ideally, try to have the green room just behind the stage separated by a curtained airwall opening or high doorway. You want to avoid green rooms on different floors (moving the costumers to the stage can be a major logistic problem), too far away (moving costumers through long hallways is also a challenge), or where the costumers have to move in view of the audience while they line up. Nearby bathrooms are a blessing.

4. Is there a way to get the costumers back to the photo area and green room easily after they come off stage?

5. Is there room for the audience to line up before the masquerade starts without interfering with general traffic or the costumers' green room?

Main Hall Layout

Start your plan with the main hall and do a rough layout considering the following.

Audience Entrances

How will you move the audience into the hall? Will you use all the doors or just a few? What traffic pattern avoids the tech equipment as much as possible?

If you have more than one door into the hall for the audience, consider having special seating line-up at the front door and fill the house for general seating from the middle or back. Special seating includes the disabled, VIP's, any available light photographers and video (signed-up in advance).

Special Seating

In the usual situation of a center aisle set-up, your first consideration is where to put the judges.

Judges Seating

Give the judges the best view in the house. They have to be able to see the presentations unobstructed and as nearly straight on as possible. Be sure you leave room behind the judges' table for them to be seated and exit easily.

If you have a center exit for contestants, put the judges' table in front of the stage just slightly to one side. It usually works best if this is on the opposite side from the main entrance side, so they get a clear view of the majority of entrances.

If you have no through-the-audience exits, then put the judges dead center in front of the stage. You can have the center aisle start just behind them.

Put these in the first rows behind the judges' table. Get a clear idea from the convention chairman as to who should be sitting here, how they will be identified and how many there are likely to be. Rope off chairs accordingly.

Available light photo and close-up video.

The seats in the front row nearest center stage and unobstructed by the judges go to photo. These should be strictly allocated and reserved by sign-up in advance. The House Manager should be informed as to who gets these seats and how those people will be identified. The first seat on the center aisle in the first few rows can also be used. Rope off and identify as photo seating.

Handicapped seating

The far ends of the front row on both sides of the aisles can be used for handicapped seating. Keep the aisles in front clear for access. You can also remove the end aisle chairs from a few rows down the center aisle for wheelchair seating. Rope off and mark these as handicapped seating.

Contestant seating

Put these wherever it is easiest to get contestants in and out without obstructing the audience's view and attention during the masquerade. A separate side section, or area in the back of the hall is best.

Lights, Sound, Video Placement

Sound: You will need a table for the sound set-up. This must have a good view of the MC, the stage and the main entrance, so the sound tech can see the cues. If this is away from the main audience entrance and exit area, the cabling will be in less jeopardy.

Lights: The lighting set-up will be dependent on the hall and stage layout You will probably want two risers for follow spots, one on each side of the hall about half-way back. Do not put your follow-spot in the back dead center or you will blind your contestants!

Video: You will want at least one video camera on a riser in center back. Optionally you may also have cameras on the side risers for the spotlights and in the special seating areas.

MC Podium

The MC's podium should be in front of the curtain screening the main entrance. It may be on the floor level or on a low riser of its own, or if you have a real stage, completely to the side. It should not occupy any of the costume presentation space, but should be clearly visible to the audience, and technical crew. It should be on the main entrance side, so that messages can be passed through the curtain from backstage with ease.

Determining The Traffic Pattern

Even before you actually lay out your stage proper, you need to determine the audience and contestants traffic pattern - how the audience will enter and exit the hall, how the contestants will get from the green room staging area to the stage, from the stage to photo, from photo back to the green room or to contestant seating.

You also need to consider everything else that will be occupying the main hall, tech risers, aisles, tables, lights, doors, etc.

Stage Layout

Start by determining the exit pattern.

Exit options

1. Center exit straight through the audience to the back of the hall.

> **Pros**: Everyone gets a view of the costumes.
>
> Easiest exit from stage for presentations. Requires no turns.
>
> No interference with next costume coming on stage.

Cons: Costumes can look clumsy coming down center stairs in full view of judges and audience.

If hall is very long, masquerade may be slowed by the length of time it takes one entry to get to the back before the next one can start.

Needs a lot of walkers to escort costumes down the aisle. Needs a wide center aisle.

Best use: in wide shallow halls where exit walk is short, or in a masquerade with comparatively few entries.

2. Center exit, then turn in front of first row of chairs and exit out first side door

Pros: Second easiest exit for presentations, only turn is at base of stairs after performance is over.

No interference with next costume coming on stage. Quick exit time.

Cons: Audience in the back never sees costumes closer than stage. Costumes can look clumsy on the stairs.

Needs wide aisle between stage and first row of chairs.

Best use: In long narrow hall, where distance to side is short or where a narrow center aisle is necessary. Also, when side exits are not possible and there are a lot of entries.

3. Exit opposite side of stage from main entrance

Pros: Short traffic pattern, quickest exit normally.

No need for costumes to descend stairs in view of audience. No time needed for costumes to transit main hall.

Cons: Presentation design more difficult.

Possible interference with next costume's entrance if two-sided entry Audience has no additional view of costumes.

Best use: when stage is very high or center exit is not possible. Also used when masquerade is very long and quick exits desirable.

4. Exit same side as entrance

Pros: Only needs pipe and drape (curtaining) for one side of the stage. Costumes do not descend stairs in view of audience.

Cons: Hardest exit to plan for in presentations

Slows the masquerade considerably, since each entry has to wait until the previous entry has completely exited before staging for its entrance. Potential for major traffic jam. •

No additional audience view of costumes.

This exit is not recommended unless no other option is available.

Staging Wings
If you have room, you should plan for staging wings on either side of the stage. These are platforms at stage height, curtained from the audience, on which an entry can get itself ready to go on while the preceding entry is out on stage. Having staging wings not only speeds up the masquerade considerably (especially when used with center exits), but gives the costumers time to arrange their costumes and assume their character, after getting up the stairs but before going out on the stage.

Stage Dimensions (if you are building your own in the venue)
The choice of stage dimensions is limited by three things:
1. The number and configuration of the risers you get from the venue or rent. Risers come in several heights and widths.

2. The size of the hall after you've accommodated everything else that has to be there.

3. The size of the masquerade. If you are staging a small local masquerade with primarily solo costumes, a smaller stage in the 12' x 18' range is better. If your masquerade usually draws couples or small groups plan a larger stage around 20'x 24' '(and be sure to have two-sided entrance capability). If you often get 8 - 12 person groups, then you'll want a stage in the 32' x 24' range. A stage much over 40' square is a lot to fill even for a Worldcon.

To Thrust or Not to Thrust
A thrust is a projection from center front. It may be one riser deep or it may extend into a longer runway.

Runways

Pros: The audience has a good long view of the costume. More of the audience gets a closer look.

Cons: Runways require longer presentations, since you have to present down the entire runway. Large costumes may have difficulty on a narrow runway.

Runways eat up seating space. Requires a center exit

Hard for judges to see entire presentation, and requires side placement of judges' table.

One-riser thrusts

Pros: Makes it easy for novice costumers to know where to present from. Gives a short walking space to prepare for a center exit.

Gives solo costumes a front and center space. Gives more options for presentation staging.

Cons: Eats up seating space

Makes a center judging table difficult. Virtually requires a center exit.

Entrances
The entrance areas should be masked from the audience by pipe and drape, curtaining or screens. These should be at least 10 feet high and preferably 12 feet, so even tall banners and props are screened. This allows the costumer to get all elements of the costume in order and "make an entrance," surprising the audience.

In addition to the staging wings mentioned above, the entrance area should have enough screened area to allow for props, backdrops, banners etc. to be arranged before climbing to the staging wing. This area also often ends up as the holding pen for unwieldly props that won't fit through the door.

Stairs
After lots of experimentation, experience has shown that the best method of getting costumes on and off a hotel-style stage is stairs. Wide shallow steps with no railing are the best. Even the largest props can be gotten on stage step by step or in the extreme case, lifted bodily by the pusher crew (or, in one case, fork lift).

And to squash what many think is an alternative to stairs: **RAMPS DON'T WORK**! Try climbing a ramp in 6" high heels and you'll see why. The taller the costume, the greater the angle of lean on a ramp, and the greater the difficulty of getting up it. Ramps have been tried several times, and always fail.

Now that you've determined your stage layout and traffic patterns, draw a neat diagram showing all relevant dimensions and publish it in the progress reports. You will also want to sketch the hall layout so the venue knows where to put things. Sample sketches of stage and hall layout are shown below,

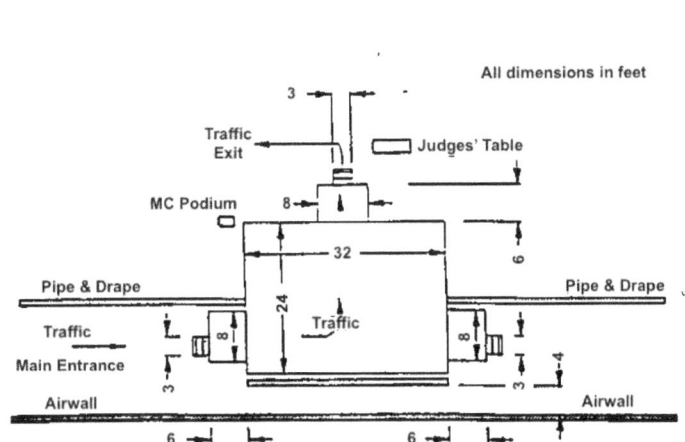

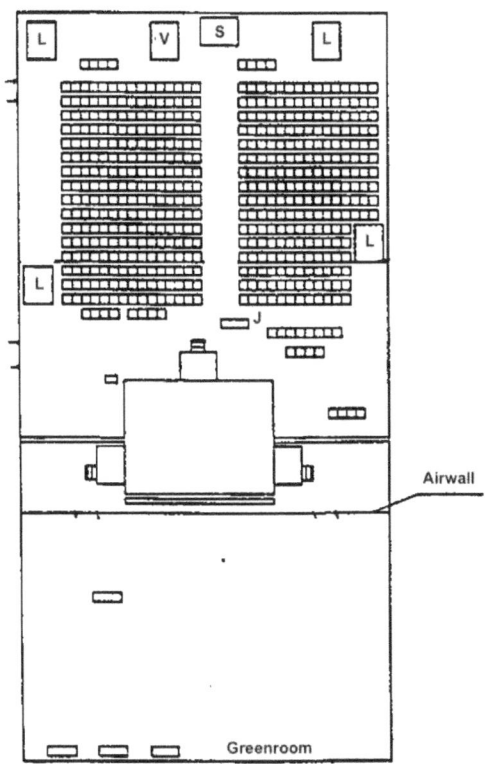

Before the contestants sign up for the masquerade, you will have to provide them with information on how it will be run. Several different information and rules sheets are included in this section so you can see how different masquerades have handled this. The wording shown below in **BOLD** type is the latest versions we have of different parts of this information, and supersedes that shown on any particular form. We suggest you review all of these and develop the format that suits your needs best. But in any event, you will need to spell out the following:

1. *Contestant information* - this covers the logistics of the masquerade: time and place, sign-up deadlines, green room location and check-in times, probable tech support, stage layout, traffic patterns, media labelling and handling, rehearsal availability if any, things a contestant should bring, backstage facilities, location of judges' table, contestant seating if any, and anything else the contestants should know to cope with the event.

2. *Rules* - these are the mandatory regulations of the masquerade, and generally cover such things as the skill divisions for judging, types of judging categories, weapons policies, fire/flame policy, time limits, restrictions on various types of costumes, no smoking areas, number of times a contestant may appear, PG-13 rating, and the lunacy clause among others.

3. *Guidelines/Advice* - these are the suggestions the Masquerade Director may make for the contestant's well-being and the smooth running of the show.

Contestant Information

At a minimum, include the following:

I. When and Where Information
   a. When and where the masquerade will take place
   b. When and where contestants should check-in (usually the green room)
   c. When is the registration deadline, and what is the deadline and location for handing in media, scripts, documentation, if different from the reg deadline.

II. Tech and Front of House Information
   a. Tech support - What will they get for lighting and sound if they don't request anything special (known as the Default Tech).
   b. If possible, tell contestants what other possibilities you can support - blackout, colored lights, colored spots, strobe lights etc. Let them know where on the entry form to indicate their wishes.
   c. Stage Information - At least give your contestants an idea of the stage size. Include, if possible, a stage diagram showing the traffic flow, main entrance, opposite entrance if any, and all possible exits. Showing the location of the judges' table and contestant seating if any is a nice touch. If you are publishing this information in a pre-con Progress Report, you should try to include any costume limiter: ceiling height to chandeliers, doorway width and height, number and size of stairs etc.
   d. Media information - Indicate acceptable formats, how you want media labelled, and where they are to be turned in. The following works for most sound set-ups:

   MEDIA: Label the media with your name and your costume name. If a cassette tape, mark the side you want played "PLAY THIS SIDE". Mark the other side "WRONG SIDE". Make sure your tape is cued up and ready to play so the sound tech need only drop it in the player and press the button. *DO NOT GIVE US COMMERCIAL TAPES CUED TO YOUR SONG.* If they accidentally get played, we will not be able to find your cuing again. Dupe the music onto separate media with only your music on it. We suggest you put your music on the beginning of both sides of the cassette tape, just in case. Leave a three second leader before the music starts. "

e. Rehearsal availability - Some conventions schedule time for full technical rehearsals before the masquerade, and this time should be noted. At a minimum, you should let people know if they will have any access to the stage prior to setting foot on it for their presentation. This may be in the hour just before the audience is let in!

III. Backstage and Photo Information

a. Den Leaders - If you are having Den Leaders, let your contestants know what to expect from them.

b. Repair Kit - If you are having one, it is wise to let contestants know that this is available, but for Emergency Repairs Only. Some contestants have been known to try to build most of their costumes out of Repair Kit supplies, if not warned.

c. Location and procedure for Judging and Official Photo (if you are having either) - Include any fee contestants will be expected to bring with them for judging photos. $1.00 is customary and the contestant gets the photo afterwards.

Rules

In the information shown below, suggested wording is shown in bold.

I. The following are generally accepted by the majority of masquerades:

a. **No fire or flame allowed on stage -ABSOLUTELY NO EXCEPTIONS!**

b. **Purchased or rented costumes may not be shown in competition.**

c. **No messy substances, wet, dry or oily, that might ruin the costume of any other contestant will be allowed in the green room or on stage.**

d. **This masquerade is rated PG-13 - please, no-flagrant nudity. Remember no costume is NO COSTUME!**

e. **Each contestant may appear only once on stage, However, you may enter more than one costume, as long as it appears on another body.**

f. **No smoking in the green room or in the masquerade hall itself.**

g. **No flash photography while contestants are on stage.**

II. For general blanket protection, always include *THE LUNACY RULE*: "**The Masquerade Director has full authority to eliminate anyone from the competition on the basis of taste, danger to the audience or contestants, violation of the above rules, or any other reason deemed sufficient. There will be no appeal.** (We've never had to eliminate anyone yet, but this protects you and the convention from real "loons".)"

III. *Weapons Policy* - Most conventions have some form of weapons policy. The Masquerade Director will have to heed the overall convention rules, but may get some exemption with provisions such as, "**All weapons appearing in the masquerade must be checked out by the Masquerade Director and must be wrapped when carried to and from the green room.**"

Here are two suggested wordings for different situations:

a. For very strict conventions:

"**No dangerous or potentially dangerous props will be allowed. This includes anything which represents a possibility of damage to the health, well-being or costumes of the other contestants, judges or audience. No sword fighting, unsheathed blades, weapons that fire any kind of projectile, real firearms, guns that fire blanks or pyrotechnics of any type.**"

b. For more weapons-lenient conventions:

"**In general, nothing will be permitted on stage that could endanger the audience, crew, contestants or judges. Due to fire regulations, no open flames, fire, flash powder etc. will be allowed - with absolutely no exceptions. If you wish to un-**

sheathe edged or projectile weapons on stage, you must first clear your presentation with the Masquerade Director prior to check-in.

Any contestant who ignores this requirement will be disqualified. We recognize the role weaponry plays in many costumes and will do everything we can to arrange a safe way for you to display it. However, safety is the paramount concern. Don't be stupid."

IV. *Additional Rules* - The following rules often appear, but there may be some circumstances in which they do not apply

    a. There will be no live microphones for the use by the contestants. Recorded music, recorded dialog, or text for the MC to read are all acceptable.

    b. Hall costumes are ineligible to compete in the masquerade. If you've worn it in the halls during the convention (except on your way to the green room), it is a hall costume.

    c. Contestants competing Recreation costumes must provide documentation for the judges. Please provide copies, not originals, of your source materials. No books, please.

V. *Time Limits*

The amount of time given for each entry varies widely by masquerade. However, the maximum time for any entry should always be stated prominently. You should also clearly state that contestants are not required to use the full time for their presentation, and whether or not the time limits can be negotiated with the Masquerade Director. Some prefer to be flexible for larger groups, or more complex presentations; other choose the simplicity of absolute limits.

Common time limits are 60 seconds for 1 - 4 persons, with 30 to 60 seconds allowed for each additional 4 persons, up to a maximum of up to 3 minutes. Longer time limits are more commonly associated with masquerades that draw complicated costumes, large groups, and big props. Masquerades whose entries are usually mostly Novices, or solos should opt for shorter time limits - 45 seconds up to a maximum of 90 secs for groups.

VI. *Judging Categories*

There are two common categories of judging in the SF/Fantasy masquerade - Original and Recreation. Both are judged within the skill division system detailed below and are based on the appearance and presentation of the costume as it appears on stage. In addition, it is increasingly common to provide for workmanship judging up-close and behind the scenes.

    a. *Original Category* - A costume inspired by a science fiction, fantasy, mythological or other original source, but whose design is the creation of the contestant.

    b. *Recreation Category* - A costume whose design is copied from a film, television, art, comics, theatrical presentation, book illustration or other medium showing at least one good view of the costume. Recreation costumes are duplicates or design adaptations of the published design work of someone other than the contestant.

    c. *Workmanship Judging* - These are for exceptional accomplishment in the crafting of a costume. Judging is done before the stage presentation takes place and is at the option of the costumer. This is the place where exquisite attention to detail can be recognized.

VII.   *Skill Division System Definitions*

The skill divisions are designed to permit those of roughly comparable skill to compete against each other. In effect this is a handicapping system to protect the less skilled from head-to-head competition with those more skilled. However, Best in Show, if awarded, may come from any adult skill level.

    a. Definition of a win: A win is a win is a win, except "Honored for Excellence" or "Honorable Mention" need not be counted. Nor do workmanship awards count for the purpose of determining skill levels.

b. For group entries, the division will usually be determined by the group's most skilled member.

c. If you are unsure in which division to enter, ask the Masquerade Director.

The current definitions of each division are given below. Afterwards, two additional variations are noted. Note: these are for local/regional conventions. The definitions vary somewhat for major conventions like Costume-Cons and Worldcons.

Junior - Costumers under the age of 13 if not part of an adult group.

Novice - Anyone who has won less than three awards for different costumes at the Novice level in SF/Fantasy competition at major conventions. A major convention is a Worldcon, Costume-Con or big regional convention.

Journeyman - Anyone who has not yet won three times at the Journeyman level at major conventions; anyone who has won three times at the Novice level; anyone not required to compete at a higher level who feels their skill level is worthy of competing as a Journeyman.

Master - You must compete as this level if 1) you have won three times as a Journeyman at major conventions, or 2) you have ever won as at this level at a major convention. Professionals (those making a significant income as costumers) are also encouraged to enter at this level. Whatever a contestant's award history, anyone may enter at the Master level if they feel their skills are worthy.

Variations:

1. Some regional masquerades have adopted an intermediate division between Journeyman and Master, called either Artisan or Craftsman. They then reserve the Master division for those who have won in the Master division at an International competition. Definitions then would be:

   Craftsman (Artisan) - Anyone who has not yet won three times at the Craftsman level at major conventions; anyone who has won three times at the Journeyman level; anyone not required to compete at a Master level who feels their skills are worthy of competing at this level. Professionals (those making a significant income as costumers) are also encouraged to enter at this level.

   Master - Anyone who has won at least once at the Master level in International competition (e.g. Worldcon or Costume-Con), or anyone who has won three times as a Journeyman in International competition.

2. Junior - if there is a large kid's class, this is sometimes split into "self-made" and "adult-made" divisions.

Advice/Guidelines

This may range from the extremely simple to the detailed. Some common advice:

In general, you may surprise the audience, but NEVER SURPRISE THE CREW!!

Please be kind to yourself before the competition. Get some sleep the night before. Register early, and turn in all your materials properly labelled. Let the Masquerade Director know what you'll need for your presentation to run smoothly. Get a lot of practice ahead of time. Don't forget to eat and drink something a few hours before you go on.

Check in on time and let your Den Leaders take care of you. If you need a sudden repair, ask at the repair table and we will try to take care of you. If you have a problem, tell your Den Leaders or the Masquerade Director. Stay in one place so you can be found when it's your turn to go on. Let the crew help you on and off the stage so you don't fall.

Let your Den Leaders take care of your excess belongings and let the catcher crew retrieve anything you leave on stage. Don't forget to stick around for the awards - it might just be your name they call! Let us know what we can do for you to make your presentation everything you want it to be.

Rehearse, rehearse, REHEARSE!!! Remember, though, this is a costume competition, not a talent show. Let them see your costume, but *Never Bore the Audience*. And don't forget - ENJOY YOURSELF!!!!"

This all seems like a lot of words, but the more your contestants know ahead of time, the smoother things will run (and the more recourse you'll have if a problem arrives). As each contestant picks up their registration form, it is a good idea to ask them to be sure to read the sheet before filling out the form. Remind them that they will be asked to sign the form stating that they have indeed read the information and agree to abide by it. If you have clearer wording, or additional things we should include, let the *Masquerade Handbook* authors or the publisher know for future editions!!

Sample Contestant Information/Rule Sheets attached:

- Loscon 17 Rules/Information
- Baycon 1988 Rules/Information
- Costume Con 8 Contestant Information
- Costume Con 8 Technical Information
- Costume Con 8 Rules

These will give you an idea of how various Masquerade Directors have put their necessary information, rules and guidelines together for various events. Since these are all old, if there is a different wording here than in the samples, please use the wording here. We probably changed it for a good reason!

TIME AND PLACE: The LOSCON Masquerade will take place in the Ballroom 1 at 8:30 p.m.

*** CONTESTANT'S CHECK-IN 6:30 p. m. ***

Registration: All persons who wish to enter the masquerade must be registered. Registration will be open on Friday from noon to 7 p.m. and on Saturday from 10 a.m. to 1:00 p.m. REGISTRATION CLOSES AT 1:00!! All forms must be completed and turned in by 1:30!

A masquerade entry form must be submitted when registering. Pick up entry forms at the masquerade registration desk. All media, instructions to the MC and tech crew, and reference materials must be handed in at the time of registration. Mark all materials with the name(s) of the contestant(s) and the title of the presentation they refer to. Cassette tapes should be labeled on both the media itself and on its storage box. Mark the side to be played "PLAY THIS SIDE" and mark the other side 'WRONG SIDE." They should be cued with three seconds of leader and ready to play. There will be a one-dollar charge for the Polaroid photo to be used at judging time.

DIVISION SYSTEM: This masquerade will be run on the standard International Costumers' Guild Division system of four skill levels: Young Fan, Novice, Journeyman, and Master.

Skill Levels:

Young Fan: a costumer under the age of 13. Such entries will be judged separately unless they are part of an adult group. Please indicate on your entry form whether the costume was made by the Young Fan or by an adult.

Novice: Anyone who has fewer than three wins for different costumes at the Novice level.

Journeyman: Anyone who has not yet won three times at the Journeyman level or feels their skill level is up to competing as a Journeyman.

Master: You must compete as a Master if you have won three times as a Journeyman/Craftsman or if you have ever won as a Master. Anyone may enter at the Master level if they feel their skill level is worthy. Professionals (those making a significant income as costumers) are encouraged to enter as Masters.

DEFINITION OF A WIN: "A win is a win is a win". Except "Honored for Excellence" or "Honorable Mention".

NOTE: For groups, the skill level of the most skilled person is the category used for the group.

Please note that any contestant may elect to compete "up" by entering at a higher still level than they might appear to qualify for. But contestants found competing "down" - entering at a lower skill level than they would qualify for - may be disqualified. If you are uncertain of your skill level, ask at Registration.

Judging will be combined for original and recreation costumes unless large enough groups of both types of costumes exist. However, be sure to check the correct category because there are variations in judging the two types.

Categories:

Original Costumes: A costume inspired by a Science Fiction or Fantasy source, but whose design is the creation of the contestant. A contestant need not wear their creation, but may use a model on stage. Be sure to note on your entry form who is the designer and who is the model.

Recreation Costumes: A costume whose design is copied or closely conceived from film, TV, art, comics, stage presentation, book illustration, or any other design showing more than one view of the costume. Recreation costumes are duplicates or close adaptations of the design work of someone other than the contestant. Those entering recreation costumes are encouraged to provide the judges with photos or photocopies of the costume source or pertinent information, since not all judges are familiar with all source media.

PRESENTATIONS: There will be no live microphones. Contestants are strongly discouraged from attempting to address the audience without one. You may turn in a narration for the MC to read. It must be typed or written in large letters on one side of the paper only, The MC will be backstage prior to the masquerade to discuss your copy with you. Another option is to pre-record words/music on media for us to play during your presentation. Turn this in when you register. Indicate that there is narration on the tape.

Contestants are urged to have at least some musical background to accompany their presentation. If you haven't brought one, you may discuss this with the Sound Tech and select one of their pre-recorded stock tapes if you like,

TIME LIMITS: Maximum time limit is 60 seconds for every 4 persons on stage; up to a limit of 3 minutes. Thus, 1-4 have 1 minute, 5-9 have 2 minutes, etc. however, shorter is better. Remember the real limit is audience attention span. DO NOT BORE THE AUDIENCE ! If your presentation is a skit, the time limit still applies! Any exceptions must be cleared with the Masquerade Director in advance. If you run over, you may be disqualified!!!

WEAPONS AND HAZARDS POLICY: In general, nothing will be permitted on stage that can endanger the audience, crew or judges. Due to fire regulations, NO OPEN FLAMES, FIRE, FLASH POWDER, etc. will be allowed. If your presentation involves the unsheathing of edged or projectile weapons onstage, you must clear your presentation with the Masquerade Director prior to contestant's call. Contestants ignoring this rule will have their presentations stopped, and they will be escorted off the stage. We recognize the role weaponry plays in many costumes and will do everything we can to arrange a safe way for you to display these with your costume. Equally, we don't want anyone hurt.

WORKMANSHIP JUDGING: In addition to the usual front- of-stage judging, contestants may choose to compete for Workmanship awards. These will be given for exceptional accomplishments in the crafting of a costume. Judging is entirely optional. If you think your costume, or some portion of it, exhibits exceptional craftsmanship, bring it over to the Workmanship judge. The standard is excellence, so there are no divisions.

TECH OR STAGING INFORMATION: Please let us know on your forms if you need any of the following: Two-sided entry, black-out or other special lighting (check to see what we can do first), special sound cues, unusual assistance getting on or off stage, unusual effects that might startle our catchers. In general, you may surprise the audience but DON'T SURPRISE THE CREW! Also note if your costumes will drastically limit your sight-lines. We will try to provide you with extra guidance.

DEFAULT TECH: This is what you will get unless you ask for something else.

1) The tree lights go to black at the end of the previous presentation and the house lights go on to let people get off at the center.

2) The house lights drop. After a five second pause, the MC reads your number and costume name. Your tape will start at the point where the MC stops.

3) The light tree comes on and the follow spot tracks you and/or others through your routine to the point where you come off the stage. The tape will stop after you are down the stairs. The spots cut, leaving only the light tree until you are off. Then they go to black and we are back at step one.

ADDITIONAL RULES:

1. Costumes worn in the halls during the day are ineligible for competition.

2. NO messy substances, wet, dry or oily, that might ruin the costume of any other contestant will be allowed in the green room or onstage.

3. Purchased or rented costumes may not be shown in competition.

4. Each contestant may appear only once in the competition. A costumer may have more than one costume entered, but they have to be on different bodies.

5. A costume can only compete in one Loscon masquerade. If you wore it last year, the audience has already seen it! This does not preclude the competition of a costume that has been worn at another convention's masquerade.

6. This masquerade is rated PG-13, Please be discreet in your use of nudity. Remember, if you're nude, Ghod gets the credit as the costume designer!

7. The Masquerade Director has full authority to eliminate anyone from the competition on the basis of taste, behavior, danger to the audience or contestants, violation of the above rules or any other

reason deemed sufficient. We've never had to eliminate anyone yet, but this protects you and the convention from the real "loons.' There will be no appeal.

SOME GENERAL GOOD ADVICE: Please be kind to yourself before the competition. Get some sleep the night before. Register early and: turn in all your materials properly labeled. Let the Masquerade Director know what you'll need for your presentation to run smoothly. Get a lot of practice in ahead of time. Don't forget to eat and drink something in the late afternoon. We will have light munchies and beverages backstage for you.

Check in on time and let your Den Leader take care of you. Stay in one place so we can find you when it's time to go onstage. If you need a sudden repair, ask at the repair table and we'll try to put you back together. If you need assistance dressing, ask your Den Leader to help. If you have a sudden problem, tell your Den Leader or the Backstage Manager.

SMOKING IS NOT ALLOWED BACK-STAGE because of the danger to the costumes and other people's lungs. If you cannot survive without a smoking break before the masquerade, tell your Den Leaders you are leaving temporarily.

When you go on, let the crew help you on and off the stage so you don't fall. Let your Den Leaders take care of your excess belongings while you are on stage. The catcher crew will retrieve anything you leave on stage and get it back to you. The take a seat in the audience and watch the show.

Don't forget to stick around for the awards – it just might be your name they call.

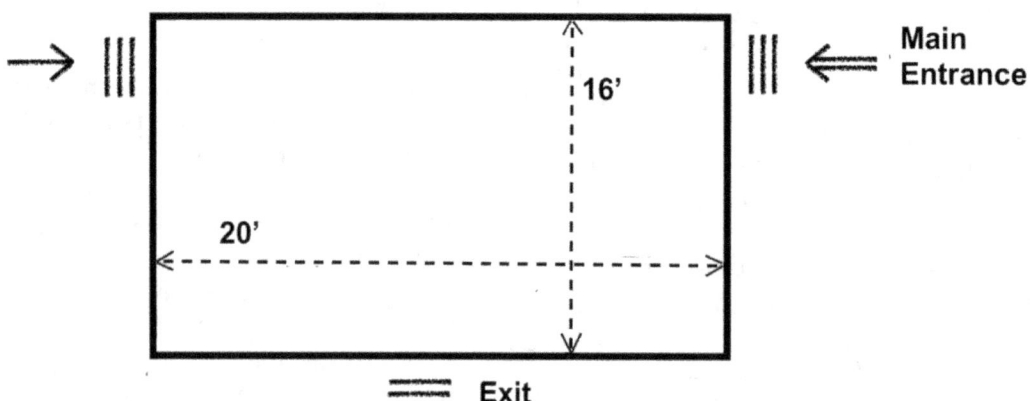

The 1988 Baycon Masquerade
Registration and Information Sheet

Time and Place:
The 1988 Baycon Masquerade will take place in the upstairs ballroom at 8:00 p.m. on Saturday evening, May 28.

Contestants Check In Time: 6:45 p.m.
Check in location: the Oak Room

Registration
All persons who wish to enter the masquerade must be registered. To register, drop off the entry form (the one attached to this sheet) in the "Masquerade Registration" box at the information desk BEFORE 2:00 SATURDAY AFTERNOON! There will be a $1 registration fee at the time of check-in.

Cassette Tapes
If you have a cassette tape to be played during your presentation, it must be turned in with your registration form before 2:00 on Saturday afternoon. Make sure the tape AND its box are labeled with the name of your presentation. Mark the side to be played "PLAY THIS SIDE" and mark the other side "WRONG SIDE". Tapes should be cued and ready to play.

Things to Bring With You
The things you should bring with you to the masquerade are: your $1 entry fee. (This is to pay for a Polaroid photo of you that the judges use for reference... you may have the photo after the masquerade), and any documentation that you want the judges to see. Speaking of documentation...

Documentation
If you are doing a re-creation costume from a movie, TV show, book cover, etc. PLEASE do yourself a favor and bring a picture of what you are re-creating as documentation. Don't expect the judges to know your source.

Divisions
Baycon '88 will be utilizing the International Costumers' Guild division system. The divisions are defined as follows:

Novice: Anyone who has not won an award at a major regional convention.

Journeyman: Anyone who has won less than three awards at a major regional convention.

Master: Anyone who has won three or more awards at a major regional convention.

For the purposes of these divisions, "major regional convention" is defined as a Baycon, Norwescon, Westercon, Worldcon, etc. Basically, any convention of about 2000 or more. Because of its specialized nature, Costume-Con is also considered in this list.

Any contestant may enter in a division higher than the one for which they qualify. For group entries, the division will usually be determined by the group's most skilled member. If you are unsure in which division to enter, ask the Masquerade Director.

Please note that there will be no separate category for re-creation costumes. Re-creation costumes will compete in the same manner as originals, using the appropriate skill division.

Presentations
There will be NO live microphone for use by contestants. Special introductions and/or voice overs may be clearly printed on the masquerade form for the emcee to read. Alternately, it may be recorded on standard cassette tape for playing during your presentation. I strongly discourage trying to speak from the stage. Please remember that this is a costume competition, not a talent show. If you wish, a tape may be used solely for background music (strongly encouraged).

If you are going to use a tape, bring it with you and turn it in with your registration forms. Make sure that the tape is pre-cued, so that all our overworked sound technician has to do is pop it into a player and push a button. Clearly label the correct side with your name (leaving room for your contestant number}, and label the wrong side as such. Don't forget to also label the tape box.

Time Limits
Presentations will be limited to 60 seconds for the first three persons in an entry; 90 seconds for up to six, and 10 seconds more for each additional person. You are NOT required to use the full-time for your presentation. If you

really need more time, see me at the convention and we can negotiate. It will take an act of Ghod for me to approve a presentation over three minutes. Remember, the time limits will be strictly enforced.

The Stage
The stage is scheduled to be 24 feet wide and 16 feet deep. The stage surface will be 3 feet off the main floor. There will be no runway. Entry will be possible from both sides of the stage if needed.

Workmanship
In addition to the regular judges, contestants may choose to compete for Workmanship awards. These will be given for exceptional accomplishments in the crafting of a costume. Judging for these awards will be done backstage, prior to the presentations. Judging is entirely optional. If you think your costume or some portion of it exhibits exceptional craftsmanship, bring it over to the workmanship judge. The standard is excellence, so there are no divisions.

Weapons
No dangerous or potentially dangerous props will be allowed. This includes anything which represents a possibility of damage to the health, well-being, or costumes of the other contestants, or the audience. No sword fighting, unsheathed blades, weapons that fire any kind of projectile, real firearms, guns that fire blanks, or pyrotechnics of any type.

Technical and Staging information
Please let us know on your entry form if you need any of the following: two-sided entry, black-out or other special lighting, special sound cues, unusual assistance getting on or off stage, unusual effects that might startle our catchers, etc. In general, you may surprise the audience, but DON'T SURPRISE THE CREW!

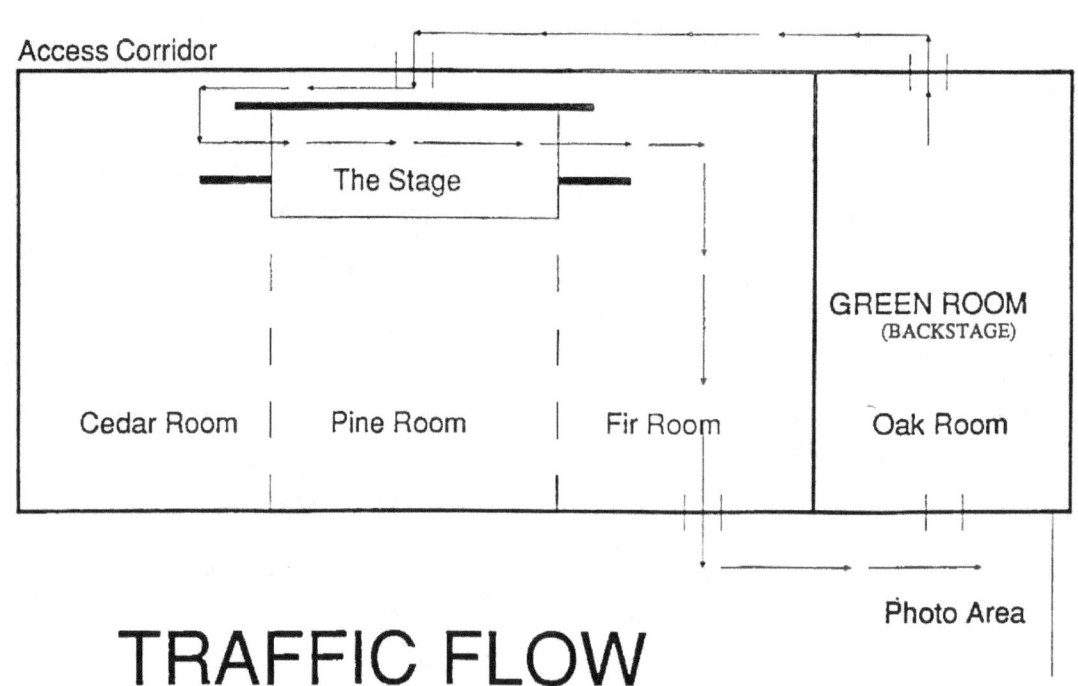

TRAFFIC FLOW

Technical Rehearsal

There will be a technical rehearsal on Saturday morning from 9:00 am to 10:00 am. I strongly encourage you to show up and at least SEE the stage and basic layout. You may practice your routine at this time. The stage will be set up throughout the convention, so you are also encouraged to practice any time the room with the stage is cleared.

The Green Room

The backstage waiting area (the green room) will be the Oak Room. We will have Den Leaders, a costume repair table, and a big-screen live broadcast of the masquerade.

Traffic Flow

When it is time for your presentation, you will go from the green room, through the access corridor, out a door behind the stage (there will be a screen so the audience can't see you), on to the stage from the right side, do your presentation, exit stage left, and proceed down the aisles to the photography area in the foyer.

Additional Rules

1. Hall costumes worn for more than one day are ineligible for competition. We strongly suggest that you not wear your costume at all before the competition, so it is fresh for the audience and judges.

2. NO messy substances, wet, dry, or oily, that might ruin the costume of any other contestant will be allowed in the green room or on stage.

3. Purchased or rented costumes may not be shown in competition.

4. This masquerade is rated PG-13. Please be discreet in your use of nudity. Remember: no costume is NO COSTUME!

5. The Masquerade Director has full authority to eliminate anyone from the competition on the basis of taste, danger to the audience or contestants, violation of the above rules, or any other reason deemed sufficient. We've never had to eliminate anyone yet, but this protects you and the convention from real "loons". There will be no appeal.

Some Good General Advice

Please be kind to yourself before the competition. Get some sleep the night before. Register early, and turn in all your materials properly labeled. Let the Masquerade Director know what you'll need for your presentation to run smoothly.

Get a lot of practice in ahead of time. Don't forget to eat and drink something in the late afternoon. Remember, we will only have water backstage.

Check in on time and let your Den Leaders take care of you. If you need a sudden repair, ask at the repair table, and we will try to take care of you. If you have a problem, tell your Den Leaders or the Backstage Manager.

When you go on, let the crew help you on and off stage so you don't fall. Let your Den Leaders take care of your excess belongings while you are on stage. The catcher crew will retrieve anything you leave on stage and get it back to you.

After the photo line, you may go into the ballroom and watch the rest of the masquerade, or go back to the green room and watch it on big-screen T.V.

Don't forget to stick around for the awards -- it just might be your name they call!

Kelly Turner
Masquerade Director

Costume Con 8
Science Fiction/Fantasy Masquerade

This competition is for costumes of futuristic, fantasy, mythological, science fiction or other original sources. It will take place Saturday night at 8 PM on stage in the main ballroom and will be judged by a qualified panel of experienced judges.

Registration Information: Registration for the SF&F Masquerade is located across from Registration and will open at approximately 12 noon on Friday, until 6 PM; and on Saturday from 9 AM until 12 Noon. Please turn in all necessary materials at the time you register; i.e. documentation, specific instructions for the tech crew, and-if applicable-your audio cassette tape.

Judging: There will be two types of prizes awarded: Workmanship and Presentation. Workmanship awards are for exceptional accomplishment in the crafting of a costume. Judging is done before the stage presentation takes place and is at the option of the costumer.

DEADLINE FOR REGISTRATION: SATURDAY NOON

Presentation awards are based on both the appearance of the costume on stage and on how well it is presented. All entrants are eligible for presentation awards.

Costumes in this competition will be judged on the Skill Division system in two categories: Original and Recreation:

Original Category: A costume inspired by a Science Fiction, Fantasy, Mythological or other original source, but whose design is the creation of the contestant. A contestant need not wear their own design(s) on stage, but may use a model or models.

Recreation Category: A costume whose design is copied from a film, television. art. comics. theatrical presentation, book illustration or other medium showing at least one good view of the costume. Recreation costumes are duplicates or design adaptations of the design work of someone other than the contestant. Those entering Recreation costumes are strongly urged to provide the judges with photos/Xerox copies of the referenced design.

SKILL DIVISIONS: These are designed to permit those of roughly comparable skill to compete against each other. In effect, this is a handicapping system to protect the less skilled against head-to-head competition with those more skilled. However, Best in Show, if awarded. may come from any adult skill level.

Junior: Costumers under the age of 13 if not part of an adult group. All kids in the masquerade must be members of the convention to participate.

Novice: Anyone who has won less than three awards for different costumes at the Novice level in SF/Fantasy competition at a major convention or international competition (Costume-Con/Worldcon).

Journeyman: Anyone who has not yet won three times at the Journeyman level at a major convention, including international competition: anyone who has won three times at the Novice level: anyone not required to compete as a Master who feels their skill level is worthy of competing as a Journeyman.

Master: You must compete as a Master if 1) you have won three times as a Journeyman/Craftsman at major conventions or international competition; or 2) you have ever won as a Master in International competition. Whatever a contestant's award history, anyone may enter at the Master's level if they feel their skill level is worthy. Professionals (those making a significant income as costumers) are encouraged to enter as Masters.

IF YOU ARE UNSURE OF YOUR SKILL LEVEL. ASK THE MASQUERADE DIRECTOR WHEN YOU REGISTER. The MD's decision is final.

The green room is located in the Grove Room, and will be immediately behind the stage, separated by an airwall from the main ballroom. Access to the backstage area will be through an opening in the airwall approximately 10 ft wide / 14 ft high. The main stage entrance will be on your left as you face the audience. Two-sided entrances are possible, and you should let us know when you register for the competitions. You will exit the stage from the center stairs. There is no other way to exit, by the way!

Stage dimensions are generous: 32 ft wide by 24 ft deep. There will be a center thrust 8 ft wide by 6 ft deep. You have from 13 ft to 11 ½ ft of ceiling clearance from the stage (the ceiling is lower in places). Your costume must however, be able to get up and down stairs three feet wide, or bring your own Gophers to lift you up and down.

☞ There will be *NO LIVE MICROPHONE* for contestants. Put all music / dialog either on tape or TYPED / PRINTED *NEATLY* for the MC to read.

Default Lighting and Sound Support: This is what you will get unless you ask for something else.

1. The tree lights go to black at the end of the previous presentation and the house lights go up to let the costumes get off to the side.

2. The house lights drop. After a 5 second pause, the MC reads your number and costume name. The tape will start at the point where the MC stops.

3. The light trees come on, and the follow spots track you and / or others through your routine to the point where you come off stage. The tape will stop after you are down the stairs.

4. The spots cut, leaving only the light trees until you are off. Then they go black and we're back at step one.

This general lighting / sound plan will make the majority of costumes look just great. We have a very experienced lighting and sound crew, who will do their best for you.

IF YOU ARE PLANNING ANYTHING UNUSUAL, HOWEVER, IT WOULD BE IN YOUR OWN BEST INTEREST TO CHECK WITH US AT MASQUERADE REGISTRATION TO SEE IF IT'S FEASIBLE. But please make sure you really, Really, REALLY know what you want and what it will do to your costume on stage. We will try to give you just what you say you want!

Definition of a Win: "A WIN IS A WIN IS A WIN"; except "Honored for Excellence" and "Honorable Mention".

Time Limits: The *maximum* time limits are one minute for every four persons, up to a maximum for any entry of three minutes, e.g. 1 - 4 persons no more than one minute, 5 - 8 persons two minutes, 8 - N persons no more than three minutes. If you feel that you need more tune than allotted by these rules, you must convince the Masquerade Director of this prior to the event!

Masquerade Weapons Policy: Weapons reasonable and appropriate to their costume may be worn on the Masquerade stage, as long as they are displayed in a safe and sensible manner. If you are planning on wielding them, you MUST clear the weapon and the routine in advance with the Weapons Master or the Masquerade Director, or you will be disqualified. No exceptions. Check the convention weapons policy for weapons that are banned totally.

There will be **NO LIVE FLAME** allowed on stage. No exceptions! Our insurance doesn't cover the liability.

Rules

1) There will be a $1.00 per entry Polaroid fee for each masquerade, payable at the time you register. The Polaroids are to help the judges remember which costume was which, and you can pick them up after the masquerade in the Con Suite.

2) These masquerades are rated PG-13-please, no flagrant nudity! (And remember--no costume is NO COSTUME!)

3) NO NOXIOUS SUBSTANCES BACKSTAGE. No messy substances, wet, dry, or oily, that might ruin the costume of any other contestant will be allowed in the green room or on stage. (The No-Peanut-Butter-or-Jelly Rule)

4) Each contestant may appear only once on stage. However, you may enter more than one costume, as long as it appears on another body.

5) Costumes previously worn in the hallways at this convention are ineligible for competition. since we are recognizing hall costumes separately.

6) Purchased or rented costumes are ineligible for competition.

7) There will be no live microphones. We encourage you to bring music/dialogue on a prerecorded cassette, or typed copy for the MC to read.

TAPES: Label the tape box and both sides of the tape with your name and costume name. Mark the side you want played "PL.AY THIS SIDE". Mark the other side "WRONG SIDE". Make sure your tape is cued up and ready to play, so the sound man need only drop it in the player and press the button.

DO NOT GIVE US COMMERCIAL TAPES CUED TO YOUR SONG. If they accidently get played, we will not be able to find your cuing again. Dupe the music onto a separate tape with only your music on it. We suggest you put your music on the beginning of both sides of the tape, just in case. Leave a three second leader before the music. If you have any questions, you can discuss them with Craig Jones, our sound engineer before the masquerade.

There will be **NO FLASH PHOTOS** during the Masquerade for the safety of the contestants. We ask all contestants to go through Official Photography in the green room before going on stage, if at all possible. You will go through general photo after you come off stage. There will be a separate photo area set up for general photographers in the Lake Arrowhead room. We also ask all contestants to stick around briefly after the masquerade ends, so people who were in the audience can get pictures too.

Registration, Running Order

-- Section 3 --

Supplies Needed:

- Entry forms
- Tech entry forms (if used), rules, and information sheets
- Sign-up sheet for reserved seating for available light photography & video sign-up sheet for general photo
- Blank paper
- Pens - lots of pens, masking tape, pencils
- Magic Markers Post-it notes Scotch tape
- Stapler, staples & staple puller, scissors
- Large box for completed forms
- 1/2" bright colored dots to mark tapes, tape boxes
- Large sign giving registration deadline, call times and location of green room volunteer sign-up sheet

Staffing:

The registration desk for the Masquerade should be staffed by a knowledgeable person during the hours it is open. This will usually be the Masquerade Director, with help from either the Backstage Manager or Operations Manager. This gives costumers someone to answer questions and to help them decide things like "What division should I enter?" or "Can I have two red spots fading to blue on a musical cue?" This also gives the Masquerade Director a chance to spot potential challenges and query the costumer beforehand.

Hours of Operation:

Generally, registration should be open sometime the day before the masquerade (perhaps noon to 5 p.m.) and be open on the day of the masquerade,, from about 10 a.m. until about six hours before start time (e.g. 8 p.m. start time = 2 p.m. reg close). If you think you are going to have a very large number of entries, you may wish to push this back an hour. Leave a copy of the rules/information taped to the table when you are not there, and a prominent note saying when reg will reopen. Don't forget to get relief to take a lunch break.

Registration Procedure:

1. Hand the contestant a copy of the rules and information sheet and ask that they read it.
2. After they read it, give them a copy of the entry form and tech form. (The separate tech form is useful for larger masquerades and/or those which are likely to draw complex entries. You probably won't need it for smaller conventions.)
3. Have them fill out the form and **SIGN THE RELEASE**. *Every member* of a group must sign the form to protect you, the convention and the venue from liability in case of injury. If someone is missing and will have to sign later, make a note on a Post-it and attach to the entry form. The top sheet of this form will have to go to check-in until all signatures are present.
4. If they have special information for the MC, and/or tech, have them put that information on a blank sheet of paper and staple it to the appropriate entry form copy. If this will be turned in later, put on a Post-it note saying "MC text missing" etc.

5. Review the form for 1) legibility (especially if using 3-part NCR forms!) 2) completeness of information 3) signatures and 4) challenges. Challenges are anything you think might give any part of the crew trouble - oversized costume, special tech cues, extra-large group, etc. Ask questions until you are sure what the contestant has in mind and what you are dealing with. Make notes on Post-its for yourself or the crew.

6. If the contestant has recorded media, ask them to turn it in before the close of registration. If it is not turned in at the same time as the form, put a "Media Missing" note on the form

7. When the media is turned in, check to see how it is labelled. Each media should be labelled with the entry title. If not so labelled, write on a strip of masking tape as needed. If it is a memory stick or CD, it should have only their recording. If it is a cassette tape, it should have one side marked "Play this side" and the other side marked "Wrong Side". Ask the contestant if the tape is cued. If not, make a note for the sound head. Put a bright 1/2" dot on the side of the tape they wish played (Do not number it yet!) and put a dot on the tape box itself. Lightly Scotch tape the media to the form temporarily.

8. Place the forms, stapled texts, attached media in the large box until it is time to order the Masquerade.

9. Tell the contestant where the green room is and what time they may show up for check-in. Be sure to tell them the latest time by which they must check-in. If you have dressing facilities available, you can mention them, as well as any other amenities you are providing. Tell them the stage will be available for rehearsal 1 1/2 hours before start time. Remind them you intend to start on time and so to be prompt!

10. For those volunteering to help out, have them sign-up on your volunteer sheet, and tell them when and where to assemble. Remind them that all crew should wear Ninja blacks and comfortable shoes.

11. For the last two hours of registration, ask your Backstage Manager to sit with you. Most of the forms will come in during the last hour, so you may even ask the Check-in Clerk to join you as well. As the forms pour in, have them checked for clarity. three-part NCR forms often have to have the information recopied on the third sheet for legibility. Check the MC texts for legibility too. Discuss any problems you see shaping up and exchange thoughts on preliminary running order and den sizes.

12. When registration closes, ask the check-in clerk to stay at the table for an hour with copies of the rules, some paper and pens and a small box for the inevitable late media/text/documentation. Let the clerk know where you will be while putting the masquerade in order, and have them call you if someone is begging to be allowed to enter late. Tell the clerk NOT to give out your room number, or you will be besieged! You can talk to the late entrant and decide whether you will graciously make an exception or not. If yes, have the entrant bring their paperwork to you immediately.

13. After reg has been closed for an hour, ask the clerk to bring everything turned in late to the room you are working in. Have them post a sign on the reg table saying "Masquerade Registration Closed - Crew Check in at X:XX p.m., Contestant Check in at X::XX p.m. in the _____ room."

After the Running Order is Complete:

1. Make sure the entry number is marked on every entry form, media, media container, documentation and MC text. If it is a cassette tape, check that the bright dot with the entry number is on the side of the tape to be played and that the box is marked as well.

2. Make sure all of the necessary information is on the running order sheet.

3. Separate the entry forms into the sets for the MC, tech, and judges, making sure that text goes with the MC copy, media, and technical instruction go with the tech set, documentation goes with the judges' set. If you are working with three-part NCR forms, the MC gets the top, most legible copy, tech gets the second copy and the judges the third copy. Be sure all three copies are legible!!

4.   Put each set in running order.

5.   Make a list for check-in of things that are missing by entry number. Put the "missing media" post-it on the tech copy of the appropriate entry; "missing text" note on the MC's copy and "missing documentation" on the judges' copy, so each knows what they will be getting later. If signatures are missing, pull the MC's copy for that entry and include a note in the appropriate place in their stack, saying "Entry form X at check-in pending signature".

6.   Put the media in numerical order in a box for the sound person.

7.   Have your Backstage Manager assign dens at this time, if they can, and note the name of the Den Leaders by the den on the running order. If not, this will have to be done when backstage is set-up and Den Leaders' names written on the 3x5 cards at check-in.

8.   Make your 3 x 5 cards. Each has the large entry number on it and the name of the Den Leaders if possible.

9.   Make at least 20 copies of the running order list. Most of the major crew plus the judges and MC will need copies. If possible, give copies to key crew heads ASAP.

10.   Assemble everything you plan to take down to the hall in neat piles for fast delivery.

11.   **NOW GO EAT DINNER!!!!** This is very important, since once you start set-up, you will not have time to eat till everything is over. If possible, take your Backstage Manager, your Operations Manager and your tech heads with you, so you are sure they get fed as well.

Now you're ready to start setting up!

by Janet Wilson Anderson

Putting together the masquerade running order is the art of creating an audience-pleasing show from the raw material of the various contestants and entries. You want to put the show together so it flows from one entry to another smoothly, with mini-climaxes, and a mix of moods. You also want to try to set each entry apart from the ones preceding and following it, to make each as memorable as possible. To put your show together, you have the guidance of the entry forms and your own knowledge of the costumers and their preferred styles.

Who Orders the Show?

Usually it is the Masquerade Director, but occasionally someone with greater knowledge of the contestants in that particular show may do it. The Masquerade Director should, however, be present, and is the ultimate responsible party. You will want privacy, a flat surface such as table or bed to spread the forms out on, pens, the blank running order sheet, and if possible, the Backstage Manager or other assistant to help with the paperwork.

What Factors Do You Take Into Consideration?

Skill Level - Novice, Journeyman, Master

Category of costume - Original or Recreation

Number of people in the entry

Any special requests by the contestant for placement

Difficult technical requirements

Dominant costume color

Humorous or serious

General type of costume

The Procedure:

1. When registration closes, count up the total number of entries in each division and category.

   EXAMPLE:

Junior	3	(1 self-made, 2 parent-made)
Novice	15	(6 Recreation, 9 original)
Journeyman	10	(8 Recreation, 2 Original)
Master	5	(2 Recreation, 3 Original
Total	33	entries, 16 Recreation, 14 Original

2. Make up your running order sheet. Across the top write Entry Number, Division, Category, Entry Name, Contestant's Name(s). Down the side, number from 1 to the total number of entries. (See sample sheet.)

3. Start with the kids. Use your judgement, but generally youngest to oldest works pretty well. Fill in the information from the entry forms onto the running order. Put the number of each entry on the entry form itself and also on both dots on any media, MC text, and documentation that may have been supplied.

4. Distribute the divisions and categories down the run order using a rough numerical equality. If one third of the entries are Novice, then roughly every third entry should be a novice.

EXAMPLE: Excluding the kids, we have 30 entries. One third are Journeyman, so roughly every third entry should be a Journeyman. There should be a Master in every group of six and the rest are Novices.

You needn't be terribly strict about it, but you do want to scatter your masters and Journeymen in amongst the novices.

So Entries 4 through 10 might look like this:

    4. Novice

    5. Novice

    6. Journeyman

    7 Novice

    8. Master

    9. Journeyman

    10. Novice

Note: at this point we have not assigned any specific entries to these numbers. We've just determined that a novice entry should occur at numbers 4,5, 7, and 10 in the show.

5.   Sort the entry forms into piles by division and by category, so you know what you're looking for. Note any with special technical requirements. You will want to try to put these far apart from each other so your tech crew doesn't go crazy.

6.   Look for any special requests for certain positions from the contestants. Requests to be late in the show or last are quite common. If you can accommodate them, fill them in now opposite the appropriate division. If you know a contestant's costume is tiring to wear, slot it in an early slot.

7.   Find the entries that think they are "humorous" and distribute them evenly through the show. Try not to put two humorous costumes back to back. Of course, you will get some surprises during the show the contestants forgot to mention, but at least try to vary the mood as best you can.

8.   Assign your Journeymen and Masters to the remaining open slots for them. These are usually the more spectacular costumes and you will want to spread them out to add sparkle to the entire show. If no one has requested it already, pick one to be your Last in Show. If you know you have an impressive group, let it have the last place. Grand Finales make good theater, and generally the larger and more complex the group, the more time they are going to need to get ready anyway! If you have more than one probable crowd-pleaser, schedule it in the middle for a mini-climax to the show.

9.   Fill in the remaining open slots by looking through each pile for the designated division on your Run Order sheet. Try for a mix of Original and Recreation, singles and groups, fantasy and SF. Avoid putting two recreations from the same medium back-to-back, or a run of similar colors or themes. Strive for the maximum mix of entries.

10.   Put the entry forms in show order and go through the show entry by entry to see if you spot any problems with the sequence. Make any necessary changes.

The Master
of
Ceremonies

-- Section 4 --

The Master of Ceremonies (MC) can make or break your show. A good one can delight the audience, make the costumes look dazzling, and give everyone a good time. A bad one can bully the audience or let it get out of hand. They can destroy presentations and fragile egos. The MC is a mix of announcer, actor, traffic cop and disembodied information source - a tough combination to find. And since MC's usually have generous egos, they can also be a challenge to select and handle.

What Makes a Good MC?

1. Takes the job seriously

A good MC cares greatly about the job and knows that the costumers are the show, and the MC is there to serve them. While they may also have a certain entertainment value for the audience, this is secondary. By their demeanor, they communicate their own respect for the show, those in it and the audience. They are also willing to spend time with contestants before the show to ensure that they are saying just exactly what the contestant wants said.

2. Has a clear audible speaking voice

The MC's primary function is to introduce the entries to the audience. At a minimum, they should be audible enough for the audience to hear the entry number, title and contestant's name clearly and consistently. Good enunciation and accurate pronunciation are important.

3. Can control an audience firmly but pleasantly

Audiences can react unpredictably, and a good MC needs to be able to guide them to proper behavior. Some people have natural authority, and audiences respond to them favorably. Avoid both the bullies and the clowns.

4. Knows when to entertain and when to play it straight

This is the hardest of the MC's skills. There is always a temptation to make jokes at the costumers' expense. Or to grab the audience's attention away from the presentation with a "witty" comment or action. A good MC resists this temptation. The MC must be capable of entertaining the audience while making announcements, explaining rules and procedures, and especially when a breakdown requires "vamping" to fill time. But they also need to be able to disappear into a disembodied voice while the contestants are on stage. Too often an MC is selected because they tells good jokes, and the show is ruined because they don't know when to stop.

5. Has some acting ability

Many presentations involve the MC, whether as voice-over, shill or actor. The contestant provides text and relies on the MC to create the proper mood, get the good laugh or set up the punch line. A certain amount of acting ability is necessary for this.

Recruiting the MC

MC'ing a masquerade is a fun job with high visibility. But because it requires special skills not commonly associated with other forms of announcing, there are not many people who do it well. The safest choice is someone who has MC'd before and who you know is competent and can be trusted. Since these folks are rare, you sometimes have to take a chance on a first-timer. Pick someone with good stage presence and who is dedicated enough to work hard with you and the contestants. Recommend that they watch lots of masquerade videos and take note of what good MC's do and what to avoid. A first-time MC will have to be briefed thoroughly on their exact duties and, as well, on the do's and don'ts of MC etiquette (see 3 & 4 above).

Briefing the MC

Confirm your MC in writing well in advance of the event. Ask her/him to come by Registration just after it closes to confirm their arrival and to get a preliminary look at the show. Tell him/her where and when to show up that evening - usually in the green room about 1-1/2 hours before showtime. Ask them to wear formal attire or if costumed, something nonobtrusive.

When Registration closes, tell your MC how many entries you have and let them know if there is anything really weird. Arrange to meet after the show is put in order to give him/her their copies for advance rehearsal.

When the MC arrives in the green room, ask the Backstage Manager to introduce them to the contestants and say that the MC will be coming around to talk to each of them. The MC should discuss each presentation, confirm pronunciation and pacing of intros, and find out any special cues or delivery desired.

After this, the Masquerade Director should provide the MC with the judges' introductions, any convention announcements to be made, and remind him/her of the traditional "No smoking, no flash photography" statements. If the MC wishes, they may provide the audience with a brief explanation of the judging systems being used - workmanship vs. presentation, original vs. recreation, novice, journeyman, master divisions. The Masquerade Director will also brief the MC on what will happen at the judging intermission and provide introductions as needed.

After the judging intermission, the Masquerade Director will find out how the awards will be given and let the MC know. The Masquerade Director will also give the MC any additional announcements that have been turned in and remind them to finish the show with thank-you's to the contestants, judges, crew, audience, and the Masquerade Director as well.

After the show, the Masquerade Director will collect all forms and award lists and warmly congratulate the MC on a job well done.

INSTRUCTIONS FOR THE MASTER OF CEREMONIES

by Richard Foss

Being an effective MC requires much more than the ability to read entry numbers and announce winners; doing the job well involves the skills of a drama coach, circus ringmaster, comedian, and talk show host. A good MC must be able to submerge their personality and take on a character when a presentation demands it, but be their affable selves when providing impromptu entertainment when a backstage problem leaves the stage empty. A really good MC will improve the show not only by that ability to shift roles in mid performance, but by making the audience sympathetic to and respectful of the costumers and crew who make the whole thing happen.

Part One: Before the Show

In some cases, facilities and scheduling permit a complete run-through of the entire show before the audience ever has a chance to spot a glitch. Fortunate and few are the MCs who enjoy this situation. For you, the schedule below can be done in a more leisurely manner.

The MC's job begins in the green room, several hours before the doors open. At that time the MC receives a copy of the forms that have been submitted by each entrant, finds a relatively quiet place, and reads them over. The MC should look over each one for the following:

Vague cuing directions

Illegible handwriting, if handwritten forms are used

Unpronounceable or extremely long names

Multiple alien, foreign or archaic words

Extremely long presentations

Presentations too complex to be practical, or that violate a basic rule of the show.

After examining every form for these or other problems areas, it is the MC's job to meet with every entrant and go over their performance. Even if the entrant has a recording, the MC must talk with them and find out how they wish to be announced, as the surprise value of some entries will be lost if the name is read beforehand. Though some MCs or Masquerade Directors make the arbitrary decision to read all costume names before the entry goes on, this practice is unfair to both the performers and audience.

For those entries that come to the masquerade with a smooth presentation clearly explained, the MC's job is easy. The MC should read the copy through out loud with the emphasis and timing that seem to be appropriate, and make sure that the presenters agree. If they don't agree, it's the MC's job to conform to their vision as best as you can. Once this process of negotiation is done, the MC should mark the form in some way so that they know that entrant has been cleared.

When the MC comes to an entry which has a poor or vague presentation - or no presentation at all - they should point out the problems and then fix them in partnership with the entrants. The most common problem is excessive length, generally by giving a long-winded dissertation on the character. The presenter should be gently reminded that a presentation which leaves the audience eager to know more, is generally more successful; it's certainly better than one in which they're deluged with information about someone they'll never meet. Remind them that having a character walk in a way that is menacing or sultry is better than just telling the audience a character has those qualities, so encourage them to work on the nonverbal aspects of their skit.

Background information not actually essential to setting the stage for the performance should be cut ruthlessly. Extremely long sentences should be shortened or subdivided so the audience is not left unraveling the meaning instead of admiring the costume and presentation. Names with multiple silent letters or more than six consonants without a vowel must have an agreed upon pronunciation. (An appalling number of fantasy authors give their characters monikers based on Welsh or Irish Gaelic names that are extremely difficult for those who are not native speakers. In any audience, there will be at least three people with different ideas about how to pronounce them, and they may all be wrong)

When the final form of the presentation is agreed upon, the MC should either change the copy on the form or reproduce it themselves so that a simple, legible version exists. That version is the one that goes with the MC to the podium.

When you've gone over all presentations with the contestants, streamlined the ones that needed it, and brought to the attention of the Masquerade Director the ones that involve open flame, peanut butter, and obscenities shouted from the stage, you've finished the prep work with the contestants. It's a good idea to take the completed forms and put them in a folder or notebook to keep them together.

Part Two: Before the Masquerade: The Stage and You

After the contestants' run-through, the next consideration is the physical stage and the MC's podium. Make sure the microphone works, is at an appropriate height, and that podium itself has a pitcher of water and a glass. Make sure it also has room for the stack of papers that you will be dealing with because juggling paperwork in tight areas at low light levels is no fun. Check to see that the podium has a working light- a flashlight can be used if no light is available, but is far less convenient. You should have a flashlight at the podium anyway, in case of light failure, but should make sure you don't shine it at the audience.

You need to resolve with the Tech Crew Head or Operations Manager, and the Backstage Manager about how you and they will communicate if this becomes necessary. Tech crew people often suggest giving the MC a headset, but this is not advisable: the crew chatter is distracting, and rarely relevant to your job. The MC needs to know when a hold-up is going to make it necessary to fill time, but neither they nor the audience needs to know the exact nature of the problem. The better solution is an assistant or stage ninja who is in contact with the tech crew and backstage, who can advise the MC when extra time is necessary.

After consulting with the tech crew, the MC should contact the Masquerade Director and check in. At this time the exact running order of the program should be finalized from start to finish. Announcements of lost items, added programs, and non-masquerade-related awards to be presented at half time should be finalized and written in proper order by the MC, and the introduction for the halftime entertainment should be established. The judges should be contacted, their order of introduction established, and the exact nature of each introduction finalized.

Note that each judge should be introduced at about equal length, and briefly - the judges are not the stars of this show. Finally, the MC should take the event schedule and the entrants forms and put them on the podium so they will be in a known and safe place. After this, the MC should rest and relax for as much time as remains before going on stage. It's a good idea to walk around or do some aerobic exercise just before going on, to reduce tension.

Part Three: After the masquerade begins

The nightmare is always there; the lights go up, the Masquerade Director introduces the MC, and a nicely-dressed person who has no idea what to say stares dumbly at the mike. It has happened. It was no fun to watch. The MC must have a prepared opening that can be delivered smoothly and with a warm, friendly style. The MC should welcome the audience to the masquerade, introduce the judges, give any introductory remarks, and recite the usual bans on cellphone ringers and flash photography. After that, it's down to business.

In a perfect world, the MC's job should be easy; give the entry number, state the class, and either lounge unconcerned as a recording rolls or give the exact presentation as worked out with the presenters in the green room. It's not a perfect world, and things rarely go that simply. Recordings are lost, entry order gets changed for reasons that are inexplicable, and other snags, visible or invisible to the audience, crop up unexpectedly. A few rules will suffice for most situations.

1.   Don't accuse anyone if a foul-up occurs. The audience doesn't need to know the exact reason for a slowdown, and if it's something embarrassing, telling the audience details will cause someone needless grief. If you feel that details should be given, do them in as positive, or at least non-judgmental a way as possible. Some MC's drop in a joke or other

canned shtick at this time. MC's who have a strong personality and assurance of their comedic or storytelling abilities can fill time beautifully, but there are two dangers in doing this. If it is done poorly, the audience can become restive and hostile to the MC; if it is done too well, the MC upstages the costumers, who will be displeased.

A few MC's can pull that entertainer personality out between entries and put it right back when the show is back on, but such skill and timing is a rarity. It is much safer for the MC to keep close to their normal character, projecting a relaxed demeanor and patience with small delays.

2.   The easiest thing in the world to do after an entry bombs is getting a big laugh from the audience with a smart remark. This violates a cardinal rule of MCing: the entrants are the focus of the show, and to be treated with respect. The sword wielder who trips over their weapon, the size 40 barbarian in size 10 spandex, the "dancer" with only a learner's permit for their legs, will all improve with experience and encouragement.

Don't ruin someone's serious presentation with a witty remark either. If they wanted humor, they'd have mentioned it in the run-through. You're there to make the costumers look good, and this is sometimes a challenge, but it's your job.

3.   If you get hecklers gunning for you, ignore them. If they start going after the costumers, frostily ask them to have some respect for the entrants. If you do this, everyone in the crowd but the hecklers will be on your side, and the hecklers will usually shut up.

The above rules will get you through most unexpected situations in the course of the regular presentations. There are always new surprises and disasters that will crop up, but if you maintain the right attitude and keep the audience on your side, you'll have no problem.

Half-Time

Half time is generally easy - you make any necessary announcements, then turn the stage over to whatever entertainers have been arranged. You should keep an eye on the half-time performers, especially if the nature of their show is a play or other staged piece.

A musician, storyteller, or juggler can add to their routine if the judges are taking their time about deciding; someone with a script can't, and if you see that the performers are near the end of a set piece and the judges aren't back, you should alert the Masquerade Director. (This is the sort of thing the Director should be watching for, but sometimes doesn't.) Among the other solutions is an impromptu parade of hall costumes, which gives the audience something to watch while the MC and the Masquerade Director frantically try to decide what to do next.

Another tactic is to invite the audience behind the scenes – tell them how many people work for how long to make the event happen, and invite them to give a round of applause for everyone who is involved in producing the show they're watching. This is a positive and uplifting way to kill a few minutes, but you should not go so far as to mention all 50 of the crew by name. (And yes, someone has done that.)

Sometimes it comes down to the Masquerade Director turning to the MC and saying, "Well, you can fill some time, can't you? It'll only be a few minutes." The MC should think very carefully before replying. Five minutes can be a very long time, and there's no guarantee that those five minutes of stalling won't be followed by five more. If you actually have a background in stand-up comedy or are very confident of your hitherto untested abilities in that field, go for it. If you have a story to tell that is in some way relevant to masquerades, costuming, or anything related, tell it.

This is a hard decision, and you'll have to go with your gut feeling and your rapport with the audience. If you don't feel you can do it and there is no alternative entertainment, then announce to the audience that there will be a pause in the show and have the tech crew cue up some music. Don't leave the stage empty without announcing that pause; make it look deliberate, even if it wasn't.

The Awards

The awards are the easiest part, and with a little preparation, can be the highlight of the show. Meet with the judges before they actually come back into the hall to make sure that you can read their handwriting, and establish the exact order of the award presentations. In this way you can avoid mix-ups between award, number and name of costume, which can be both embarrassing and confusing. The rest is easy - the reading of award titles and their recipients. If one of the judges does this, just introduce them and step aside.

The only problem with this part of the show can be timing, usually a delay when a winner is at the back of the hall in a wide costume and can't move quickly. In some cases, the winner is out of the hall altogether. In such cases, allow a reasonable amount of time, and then read the next winner. The MC and Masquerade Director should have already finalized such details as whether the award certificates or trophies will be presented immediately or later, and whether all winners should stay on stage.

Summary, or So Why Does Anyone Do This?

This may seem to make MCing sound like a nightmare. If you go into the job with only a hazy idea of what you want to do, and without the skills to carry it off, it can be. The challenge and joy of being the MC is the opportunity to make the whole show run well, to assist in creating the many moods of a good masquerade.

A good MC is the ringmaster, someone who can't ride the elephants, tame the tigers, or swing on the trapeze, but makes each stunt somehow more wonderful and death-defying by introducing them with flair. The MC controls the pace and character of the show, and as much as any one person, personifies the convention and the costuming community. On nights when it all goes smoothly, the physical and emotional rush you experience when it's all over is incredible. To every person who ever tries their hand at this demanding and rewarding job, I wish you good luck.

To Start the Show

- Welcome to the _____ masquerade!
- Reminders: There is to be no smoking in this hall.
- For the safety of our contestants, please, no flash photography. We do, however, encourage you to express your appreciation for what you see on stage. Hearty applause will be welcomed!
- [ ] *Other announcements (attach list)*
- There will be _____ entries to entertain you and they will be competing in different skill levels and categories which you will hear me announce.
- *(Judging system divisions and categories)*
    [ ] *will not be explained*
    [ ] *will be explained briefly*
    (Junior = under 13, Novices = beginners, Journeymen = intermediate, Master = advanced costumers. Two kinds of judging - what they see from the stage = presentation, and skill in crafting costumes = workmanship, and two different groups of judges)
- The judges...
    [ ] will be introduced with bios (*attach*)
    [ ] will be introduced by name only
- The workmanship judges are: _____ (*or attach*)
- The presentation judges are: _____ (*or attach*)
- Now, on with the show....
- Entry number one in the _____ class.....

After the Last Contestant Has Left the Stage

- That concludes the presentation portion of this masquerade, but please stick around.
- [ ] *Other announcements*
- While the judges go off to deliberate, there will be:
    [ ] Half-time entertainment...
        [ ] entertainment is: _____
        [ ] *will start after a formal announcement (attach)*
    [ ] will start seamlessly from the masquerade.
        [ ] half-time costume walk-through...
        [ ] for award winning hall costumes only   [ ] all hall costumes
    [ ] costumes should come to the _____ side of the stage to go on.
- [ ] *Other events* _____

After the Judges Are Back

- I see the judges have returned, so if you will all take your places, we will begin announcing the winners.
- Before we begin, a few more announcements:
    [ ] winners can pick up their award certificates at _____
    [ ] media, documentation, and judging photo picked up at _____
    [ ] video replay takes place at _____

[ ] there will be a masquerade post-mortem _____

[ ] *other announcements, including after-masquerade events (list)*

- And before we announce the winners, please join me in a big round of applause for all our judges to thank them for their hard work.
- [ ] Any special awards? (*read list*)
- Now for the Presentation awards (*read list or introduce judges to present them*)
- And now for the Workmanship awards (*read list or introduce judges to present them*)
- Congratulations to all the winners and thank you to all the contestants who shared their work with us.
- Before we close, however, we would like to recognize those who made this show possible.

    Tech crew headed by _____with

    Lights _____

    Sound _____

    Video _____

    Backstage crew headed by: _____

    The front of house crew, catchers and pushers

- And the person who has made this whole show happen - our Masquerade Director _____

Operations,
Front of House

-- Section 5 --

The position of Operations Manager is a relatively new one. As masquerades have gotten more technically demanding and the coordination among various elements of the front of house work more essential, this position has come into being. In a nutshell, the Operations Manager oversees:

- The tech crew - lights, sound, video
- The management of the front of house - traffic, security, seating, stage set-up, seating set-up, judges' table and podium
- The catcher crew
- The photography area

The Operations Manager is responsible for the layout of the front of house. With the Masquerade Director, they should visit the site and carefully map out the room. All dimensions should be noted, including height to the lowest part of the ceiling. Door heights and widths should be measured as well as any other limiting dimensions between the planned backstage green room and the stage, and in the stage exit traffic pattern. Locations of power outlets and all room lighting controls should be noted.

The Operations Manager should confirm the items available from the venue: types, number and dimensions of risers, podium (with light?) and microphones, pipe and drape if any, type of power available, tables and chairs. They should also find out if it's a union house, and to what extent the venue staff will be doing set-up. If you are planning to tap into the venue video for broadcast viewing, now is the time to find out how this will work.

With the Masquerade Director, the Operations Manager should determine the stage layout and contestant traffic pattern. They should also determine the audience's traffic pattern, reserving one entrance for special seating if possible. They should determine the location of the podium, judges' table, aisles and special seating areas. A rough sketch of this should be drawn up for discussion with the tech staff.

The Operations Manager is responsible for choosing and supervising the tech crew. They should meet with the tech head(s) and tell them what facilities they will have from the venue. With the rough layout in hand, they should discuss what equipment will be needed to provide adequate lighting and sound. Then they should work together to lay out the location of spotlights, sound table, light trees, video risers, and any other tech equipment that will need special facilities.

After this discussion, the Operations Manager draws a tight diagram of the layout of the front of house, indicating what set-up will be required by the venue, where everything goes, and by when it needs to be ready. A copy goes to whoever is handling liaison with the venue. They also draw up an equipment and supplies list, indicating whether items will be lent, rented or bought.

At this point the Operations Manager develops the Operations budget. This should include rental of the stage risers, podium, pipe and drape and other risers if not available from the venue. It includes all the tech equipment that has to be rented, and the transportation cost to get everything there. A budget for security badges, crew IDs, judges' table supplies and an incredible amount of duct tape and other tape should be included. This budget is given to the Masquerade Director for inclusion in the overall budget for the show.

The Operations Manager needs to recruit a Front of House Manager, if the convention is not separately providing one. They also need to recruit someone to head up the stage set-up and catcher crew and people to handle the photography area(s). Each should have a clear understanding of their areas of responsibility.

About two weeks in advance, the Operations Manager or their designee should make sure all rented items are on order and available. A timetable for equipment pick-up and delivery should be assembled. The wise Ops manager will reconfirm with the venue liaison that nothing has changed in set-up or its timing.

About a week out, the Ops Manager will be assembling their own kit of supplies and tools necessary for front of house and stage set-up. They will contact the Front of House Manager to find out about any special VIP needs they may not have been aware of. They will contact the Catcher

Head to see if catcher recruiting has progressed properly and the heads of photography to see if they have arranged for the needs of their areas.

When the Ops Manager arrives at the venue, they check in with the Masquerade Director and learn of any last-minute changes. They check with the venue liaison to reconfirm set-up times and layouts. They find the tech heads, Front of House Manager and catcher crew and set the final call times for each area. This should be posted near Masquerade Check-in, so the crews for each area know when to come.

They make sure all equipment rented or lent has arrived and is good working order. If no set-up can begin until late on the afternoon of the masquerade, they help out the Masquerade Director until set-up time arrives. They will probably also be recruiting and briefing fill-in crew. They will get the running order copies, tech forms and media from the Masquerade Director as soon as they are available. They then assist the tech heads with turning these into light and sound cue sheets.

Once set-up begins, the Operations Manager directs the efforts of the stage set-up crew primarily, and solves whatever set-up problems the tech crew may have. They assign crew to the Front of House Manager for roping off special seating. They confirm that the Front of House Manager has a responsible ballroom check-in clerk to hand out ID's and confirm special seating assignments. They check the location of the podium and judges' table. They discuss the position and number of catchers and ushers with the Head Catcher.

As the stage set-up completes, they tell the Head Catcher to let the Backstage Manager know that contestants may now rehearse on stage. If set-up is early in the day, they will coordinate the technical rehearsal with the Masquerade Director and tech heads.

The Operations Manager will also serve as the ultimate head of ballroom security. The Front of House Manager is responsible for making sure everyone in the ballroom during set-up is properly ID'd, and that door security is in place, but if a question arises, it is the Operations Manager who takes ultimate authority on ejecting intruders.

At 20 minutes to show time, the Ops Manager asks the Front of House Manager to station ushers and catchers. The Ops Manager advises them on any aisle obstructions they should tell the audience to watch for. Fifteen minutes to show time, if everything is ready, the Operations Manager advises the Masquerade Director and the tech heads. They tell General Photography to stop now, until after the contestants start coming off stage. The Masquerade Director may order the doors open for seating at this time. As the audience files in, the Operations Manager keeps an eye out for trouble areas. After the audience is completely seated, they check with the tech heads to see if they are all ready to go. If so, they advise the Masquerade Director that it is five minutes to show time. When the Masquerade Director says, "start the show" the Operations Manager gives the signal.

During the masquerade itself, the Operations Manager should station themself near the main tech table. They are there to solve on-the-spot problems if they arise. If all goes well, they can watch the show proceed smoothly. If the podium lamp blows out or a cord comes unplugged or a medical emergency arises, etc., it is their responsibility to get the problem taken care of.

During the judging intermission, they make sure that the front of house remains orderly. They solve any new tech problems, and work with the Front of House Manager to insure orderly traffic flow and unobstructed aisles. When it is time for the awards to be announced, the Masquerade Director will tell the Operations Manager. They will tell the Front of House Manager so an announcement can be made outside in the halls and people returned to their seats. They let the tech crew know so lights and sound are ready to proceed. They check that a catcher crew is back on station to assist people up and down the stairs.

After the awards are over, they supervise tear-down and pack-up. They note if any rented or borrowed equipment has been damaged. They sign any volunteer time cards. They warmly thank everyone who has helped out. They ask the tech heads, Front of House Manager and Head Catcher to pass on any suggestions for doing things better next time. They attend the masquerade post-mortem and learn for the future.

After the convention, they return all rented or borrowed equipment. They submit the bills for reimbursement. They compare their actual expenses to their original budget and congratulate themself on a job well done!

Front of House Manager - (4) - Takes care of the front of house and all non-tech crew (gofers, catchers, ushers, security, ballroom check-in). This is a job that can be improvised on the spot if the person is experienced at masquerades in any major capacity. They must be able to assert authority to control seating problems and anyone who just wants to be where they are not allowed. They will interact with security a fair amount. This person controls traffic during seating and the orderliness of the house overall. They spot the catchers and contestant ushers to ensure the contestant traffic flow is unimpeded, if the Head Catcher does not.

Depending on the type of con and number of non-costuming related events, this person may be appointed by the con committee and have a number of other duties besides the masquerade. If this is the case, it can be beneficial to issue a letter (in conjunction with the Masquerade Director) defining what is needed and when.

Judges' Clerk(s) - (2) - The judges' clerk is in charge of the judges' paperwork and recording the awards. If the masquerade has a lot of entries, two clerks will be needed. The clerk takes charge of the judges' forms, documentation and judging photos from the Masquerade Director. The clerk is responsible for the judges' table and makes sure that the judges have the right form and documentation as the show progresses. Depending on the scoring system used, the clerk may total the score for each entry. During the judges' deliberations, the clerk keeps track of all awards given, and keeps the paperwork in order. Afterwards the clerk makes sure that all the forms, papers and a complete list of the awards are given to the Masquerade Director.

Since the clerk hears all the judges' deliberations, the person that fills this position needs to be carefully selected. At smaller cons this may be a general gofer, but the judging at large cons may get very political. If possible, have the Masquerade Director pick this person. They have a better idea of the politics involved. If you assign this person, they should be closed mouthed and organized enough to assist and not hinder the judges.

Ballroom Check-in - (2)- This person handles the check-in of all workers in the ballroom, including security tagging tech and catchers. The judges' clerk or one of the catchers can act as their assistant before the masquerade. Once the house doors open, they become part of the general crew for front-of-house.

Catcher/Pusher Head - (4 or 3) - Sets up catcher and pusher crews, helps handle stage setup beforehand. This person may also be the Sergeant-at-arms who stages the contestants. Their expertise at moving contestant traffic will help determine how smooth the masquerade seems to the audience.

Catching may be a separate department from front of house depending on the level of experiences between House Manager and Head Catcher. They may also be the one spotting the contestant ushers (or walkers) in the aisles. The experienced catcher knows the other catchers and who is good and bad. Let them pick their people.

Catchers/Pushers - (2) - Catchers help people off the stage and through the aisles; pushers help get people onto the stage and retrieve anything left on the stage. Both should be dressed in ninja black from head to toe, in low shoes and in something they can squat in.

None of the crew should be wearing elaborate hats or sleeves or anything else that might interfere with the masquerade costumes. They do not have to be large; a few nimble small people are needed for things like stage clearing. Some people want to be catcher who are not appropriate or not suitably dressed; give these people to the House Manager for ushers. If you need more people back stage, give them an option. Many elect to stay in the house where they can see the whole masquerade.

Traffic Control & Ushers (aka walkers) - (1) - Before the masquerade these people help keep un-authorized personnel out of the ballroom. You will need one at each door to check those entering. If they have legitimate business with the masquerade, the ushers direct them to ballroom check-in for their badges. Surplus ushers and those who will be walking contestants down the aisle help with set-up before the masquerade. When the doors are open, the ushers insure an orderly flow of people into the ballroom. One usher directs those who have special seating privileges to the proper area. After the audience is seated, the ushers take places along the main traffic pattern and escort the contestants to photo, greenroom or assigned contestant seating, depending on the traffic plan. If there is assigned seating for the contestants, one or two ushers will need to be stationed there throughout the masquerade to assist the costumers in getting seated and out again for awards.

When the judges leave for their deliberations, the ushers quickly move into the aisles and to the doors to help people who wish to leave do so. They remain on their stations throughout the halftime to keep the house orderly. When the judges return, they return to their masquerade posts.

After the awards are given, the ushers once again move to the aisles and doors to help people exit. When the audience is mostly out, the ushers help with tear-down. They stay until they are excused by the Front of House Manager or Operations Manager.

Supplies

Depending on the con you will get your supplies from backstage or from the tech crew

- Copy of running order

- Pipe and drape

- Many rolls of duct tape

- Christmas tree lights

- Extension cords

- Neon tape

- Pen lights - one for each entrance, and at least two for the aisle walkers

Duties

Usually, the catchers and pushers are the set-up crew for the front of house, except for tech. They switch hats just before the show starts and then turn into the teardown crew after the show ends. The Head Catcher/Pusher takes direction from either the Operations Manager or in some cases, the Front of House Manager. You will be recruiting a lot of crew on site, so you should show up at masquerade registration periodically to get volunteers. You should remind them to come dressed appropriately.

Eat in the afternoon before set-up starts. You will be working for many hours and will need all of your strength!

Wear black, tight, comfortable clothes and shoes. Remind your crew to wear the same. Most of them will be sitting or squatting during the show and doing set-up and teardown; comfort is key.

Find out when the stage is going to be set-up. If it's a rented stage, crew call will be much earlier than if the venue is setting up the risers for you. Have as much of your crew as possible there ahead of time to help. Find out from the Operations Manager if the venue is union. They can get annoyed if your people move risers that only union people may touch.

Find out from the Operations Manager the design and exits of the stage so that you can determine how many catchers you will need and where to place the biggest catchers. Will there be two-sided entrances? If so, you'll need more pushers. Is there a way for contestants to get from one side of the stage to the other via a service corridor? Then you'll need walkers in that corridor. Or do contestants have room to cross behind the back pipe and drape. If so, they will probably need a walker there to help - one with a pen light to light the way in the dark. What is the traffic pattern after contestants leave the stage?

Take directions from the Operations Manager on setting up the stage and the front of house. Tape extensively. Tape the riser seams so that costume trains will not snag. The uneven partitions should have many layers of duct tape so that the surface is safer. Tape the stairs to the stage. Are there any places likely to snag high heels? Tape the area heavily so that a small heel will not likely go through. Put neon tape arrows down the aisles following the contestant's exit path.

Once the stage is set up, and if it is made of risers, personally check out its stability. Go to each and every block. Have your biggest crew member jump and push on them. If any are unstable, now is the time to have them replaced. If the stage is very uneven and there are no other pieces, can the bad blocks be moved to an unused corner? When you know all your problem spots, let the Operations Manager know. See what you can work out with them to fix the worst problems. Warn the Backstage Manager of anything that can't be fixed, so an announcement can be made to have people avoid those spots.

NOTE: If the stage was set up before you arrived, do not remove any tape marks that were already there. If risers must be moved after the stage has been set up for any time, make sure to notify the Backstage Manager as early as possible. Contestants will need to remark the stage.

If Christmas lights are going to ring the stage, have them taped to the edge of the stage, pointing down so they don't snag costumes. Tape down all extension cords around the stage and on the floor of the ballroom. Use a strip of neon tape to mark across each riser of all the stairs. Tape a large 'X' in the center front of the stage with the neon tape, so the costumers know where the prime stage position is. Put neon tape markings on any cords that cross main traffic paths, in addition to duct-taping them down.

After the stage is done, set up all pipe and drape. Tape their bases down securely. Use small strips of tape to secure the side seams. Leave one side seam untaped on both sides, so people can get back and forth behind the stage.

When you are set up enough on stage for contestant run-through, let the Backstage Manager know. (Tech, sound, lights and drape do not have to be ready. Cords can be stepped over.)

After set-up is complete, brief your crew on where they will need to be and what will be expected of them. Show each person their station and ask them to be in that station when the doors are open for seating.

You will need at least two pushers on each entrance. If you know you have some large props or costumes to lift onto the stage, assign some extra folks. Find out if contestants have their own roadies to handle these and let them do it. Find out if they are going to remove them as well. (Surprisingly often, they don't think of doing this!) At least one pusher should be trained to gently "floof" trains, trailing draperies, capes and such. As a costumer starts up the stairs, one pusher should guide them by the hand if possible, and the other should lift away any costume bits that might be stepped on.

Assign a nimble pusher stationed on the opposite entrance side to the stage clean-up job. This person will pick up anything dropped on the stage during a performance, and if it is a costume piece, see that it gets to the contestant before they reach photo. If you have lots of volunteers, you may station a runner to take the articles to the costumer.

You will want to station a catcher about every six feet around the edge of the stage. Remind them to stay low so they don't obstruct the audience's view. Tell them it is an honor to have a costumer fall on them, but a greater honor to keep them from falling in the first place!

Put two big, athletic catchers on the main exit. These are the people responsible for getting the costumers safely off the stage and down any stairs. Put fairly big folks at the two closest side catcher spots so they can pitch in if you have to move a whale.

The stair catchers should wait until the costumer clearly indicates they are done and ready to exit before standing up and reaching for their hands. After they hand the costumer down the stairs, they should hand them physically off to an usher with a pen light. Be sure you have enough ushers or walkers to escort every costume completely through the aisles to their next station. You will need at least two or even three walkers if the way is long.

About 15 minutes before start time, go backstage with your running order. Quickly check out each entry for probable entrance/exit challenges. Note them on your running order so you can advise the main exit crew or assign extra staff. Let the stair catchers and pushers know which entry numbers have serious challenges (blind, big feet, wheels, wide skirts, etc.) so they can be ready to assist. Return backstage to assist with lineup.

Five minutes before show time, check to see that everyone is in position and that all the costumers are lined up ready to go. If you are going to be Head Pusher, station yourself so you can check each entry's 3 x 5 card for the correct number.

After the presentations are through, listen to the MC to see if there will be anything going on during half time requiring you to get people on and off the stage (such as convention awards, or hall costumes). Have your people stick pretty close to their stations so they can go back into position as soon as the judges return. Help the award winners up and down the stairs, no matter where they come from.

After everything is over, ask your crew to help with tear down. Remember to thank everyone of them profusely for their assistance, and make notes of those you want to work for you again. Lastly, check with the Masquerade Director or Operations Manager for any last instructions. Then go party after a job well done!

You will be doing three jobs. Before the masquerade starts, you will be asked to help with setting up the stage and pipe and drape. During the masquerade, you will help contestants. After it's over, you get to tear it all down again!

During set-up and tear down, you will be working under the direction of the Head Catcher/Pusher and the Operations Manager. Just pitch in and do whatever needs doing. Make sure you know what time stage setup will be. Your help is needed for this event. Make sure you arrive on time because there is a lot of work to do in a very short time period. Be sure to pick up your masquerade security badge when you enter the ballroom.

As a pusher or catcher, your job will be to assist contestants on and off stage. Also, you may be required to place or remove props and accessories on or from the stage.

You must dress completely in black with comfortable quiet shoes.

Your outfit may have no sleeves that can interfere with the contestant costumes and you should not wear any kind of a hat that will obstruct anyone's view. A number of catcher positions may require crawling around or behind the stage. If you are not dressed appropriately, you will be assigned to another job.

Shortly before the start of masquerade, the Head Catcher will assign you to a position. You may be assisting a person up the stage and helping them arrange the train of their costume; you may be assisting them off the end of the runway when the spotlight is blinding them; you may be positioned at an inside corner ready to catch a contestant who misses their mark; you may be the person who removes all the items left on stage when a contestant leaves; you may be on the floor in front of the audience ready to assist the contestants out the final door; or you may be walking contestants down the aisle with a flashlight etc.

During the masquerade, remember to talk only when absolutely required and even then, to keep your voice very low. If you are a stage catcher, remember it is an honor to be fallen upon by a costumer, but it is an even greater honor to keep them from falling in the first place! Safety is your primary function!

If a group of contestants has its own roadies, and they want to put them on and off stage themselves, get out of the way! Their group has a better idea what on the costume will snag and what the sight lines are within the costumes.

During half time, hall costumes often go on stage. Be prepared to assist these people or anyone needing to go up on the stage. When the awards are announced, the contestants will be coming on stage from any of the entrances or exits. Be prepared to direct them to the right part of the stage. This is a point where you must be very careful. The contestants are often rushing at this point, exhausted and excited. Be very careful of their trains and that they are not too close to stage edges. After the masquerade is over, stay and help break down the stage area. (Most parties take an hour to set up after masquerade is over anyway.)

For all your hard work, you will usually end up with one of the best views in the house!

Tech

Lights, Sound, Video

-- Section 6 --

The masquerade technical areas are: Lights, Sound, and Video. Although the last is relatively new to general consideration, as more masquerades are recorded and/or shown live for out-of-hall viewing, it has become more important. All of these areas are to some extent venue-dependent. There have been masquerades which have had the luxury of a full stage setup. Most have to make do with hotel ballrooms. They all share the concerns and to some extent the organizational and procedural needs described below, even though the primary orientation is the hotel ballroom based midsize con.

Organization

Organization will depend to some extent on the size of the masquerade. (See the Organization Chart). A medium-to-large masquerade will need a Lighting Head, a Sound Head, and a Video Head. Sometimes the Photography Head is also under tech. Each will need one assistant at a minimum, with the lighting crew consisting of one person for each manned light station (follow spot or lighting control - and don't forget the room light controller), one emergency replacement on standby for each three crewpersons in service, and the video crew - one camera person per camera station, and one controller to ride herd on the freelance videographers.

In general, the heads of departments will run the main control station for each, and the Operations Manager will do the overall coordination and disaster relief. During setup the Operations Manager acts as the venue liaison, is usually involved in the pipe-and-drape mess, and deals with Concom to supply crew if necessary.

An experienced Operations Manager will already have done most of their crew setup before the con, and will snag willing passersby if they are known or vouched for. Just making do with gophers from gopher central is usually a recipe for disaster (not always - some good people come out of that - but usually not). This is not due to bad people as gophers, but to the need for a fair number of experienced crew with a few newbies, not the other way 'round.

This organization extends to the communications net. The basic minimum net has the Lighting Head, the Sound Head, the follow-spot operator(s), the room light controller if remote from the lighting control panel, the Backstage Manager, the Operations Head, the Masquerade Director, the Video Head, and the Front-of-House Manager on it. That is 9 to 10 sets. Priority is roughly in the order given, but this must be examined for each case. The cheap little 49 MHz radio headsets will work, at the risk of interruptions, but it is far better to get the real radios the con can rent. And usually has, for the security people. If you must use the little sets, try to get enough on the same frequency so that the communications setup doesn't actually impede progress. And if you have wired comm, such as at a real theater, cord length and station is important.

Procedure

There are three different procedural sequences: pre-masquerade, masquerade operations, and teardown.

Pre-masquerade

The pre-masquerade starts months before the con, with the setting up of the organization, arrangements for equipment rental (and its handmaiden, budget crisis), tech layout (using the stage layout hopefully available), and fighting with the Concom for enough setup time. A set of default values are made up (this is adequate for about 80% of most costumes) for lighting and sound. Video arrangements are set. At a large con, such as Worldcon or some Westercons, all this will be mailed to the preregistered entrants. At smaller cons, this is present at the signup table, and the table gopher primed to tell entrants that if they aren't really sure of their staging, to use the defaults. In any case, the masquerade pre-meeting will establish the requirements for the entrants.

The next flag is just before the con, where equipment is rented, transported to the con, and either stashed or set up, depending on the other uses for it. This will require four to five people and a truck or large van. The Lighting Head is usually in charge of this, since they are also the most likely to know if you are getting potentially defective equipment. Most audio techs bring their own and rent one or two items, such as big speakers or a master control board. The chief difficulty here is to tread the narrow line between too little equipment and too much (or too expensive). (See Equipment, below.)

The next event is getting the Heads together for a review meeting, where the Masquerade Director and the Operations Manager give them the latest master stage plan, and they can discuss how silly the master plan is, divvy up setup responsibilities and schedule, and get acquainted.

Next, if the time and circumstances permit, is tech rehearsal. For a very small con with no elaborate costumes, this is often done as a quick informational and cue-checking session between the tech crew and the interested contestants. Better than nothing, but inadequate for any sort of complex cuing, or for color balancing and fading or spot selecting with the lights. Ideally, the stage with the lights and sound setup are available the night before the masquerade, and the entrants who need rehearsal and the crew meet and go over the presentation, working out the bugs. The chance to do this is very rare, and usually only an extra hour or so before the start of the masquerade can be squeezed in. It is certainly worth trying to get advance setup, however. Even if setup is not possible, a mandatory meeting of some kind is necessary, and the lights and sound head techs should be there.

Starting about three hours before the masquerade, or two and a half if you have a very experienced crew or a small con, actual setup begins. This is where the entire crew, as well as recruits for such tasks as pushers, catchers, as well as people recruited specifically for setup, are given copies of the master plan, told who to report to, and set to work doing things.

Emphasize safety. They will be setting up light trees, follow spots, and pipe-and-drape. Big, heavy stuff with fall potential. Keep all nonessential personnel out of the way. Sandbag everything that even looks like it might fall. Tape down all wires, and route to keep them out of the traffic pattern for either the audience or the entrants. Place and test speakers and mikes, and balance the room. Place and test light trees and follow spots, balance lighting and test controller board. Set up video camera positions and controller board (if any). Do video light check, set up link to backstage monitor for entrants. Do communications check (if you have the 49 MHz radios, look out for baby monitors and other things which shouldn't really be on this frequency but sometimes are) and parcel out radios. Check again for un-taped wires, vulnerable power plugs, etc. Station the tech crew to keep the audience from crashing into anything upon entry. Give entry OK to the Front-of-House manager. Duck.

Masquerade

This is the critical phase of the operation. If setup and preparation have been done correctly, if the equipment works, if the personnel are experienced and not prone to hysteria, and if no actual disasters take place, it will flow smoothly. It is hard enough to achieve good technical production values in an unrehearsed setting with limited equipment, a team which has just come together, and surprise staging. To add to this by not trying to prepare properly is nearly impossible.

At this time, there should be copies of the tech sheet with annotations in the hands of the Lighting Head, the Sound Head, and the Video Head, as well as any tech crewperson who is not on the net. The Tech Director, who may be any one of the above, is going to direct the crew from these sheets and from the changes put out over the net by the Masquerade Director, the Operations Manager, the Back-of-House Manager, or other person directly involved in the operation. Last minute changes, sudden emergencies ("Great Ghu, the Wookie" just lost their paw - substitute number 17!) and the exigencies of traffic flow will affect the pacing and the order, or even the existence, of the entries. This is where the calmness of the Tech Director is paramount. Even a small amount of hysteria will ruin a masquerade.

The standard sequence is: from black, cut to MC, MC reads number, class, and name of costume (MC should have podium light), soundtrack starts and light trees come up, dim spot illuminates entrant(s) as they enter, follows until they finish, light trees dim, bring house lights to half if center exit is used (otherwise, can just go to black and wait), go to black, next costume. This has many modifications and variations depending on the situation, but the basic sequence idea is to call attention to the costume during the time it is on stage and not while entering or leaving.

After the run through, the judges retire, and halftime begins. There will be a lot of audience movement, so some measures may be necessary to protect light trees and/or power/signal wires. If the tech crew is called on to remain functional for entertainment, then the catcher crew can do some of this, if the Operations Manager has arranged for it.

Typically, there will be some slack time. The sound tech will, most likely, have a selection of music for fill in, ranging from background for hall costume show to "Timewarp" for livening things up. Avoid loud stuff and heavy metal – it drives the audience out and results in much fewer people staying for the awards.

After the judges return, the awards are presented. The lighting people can now relax (this calls for room lights and only the follow spots) but the sound tech gets a workout. Craig Jones, the master of the quick hands, could hear the announcement of an award and have the media from that presentation playing before the entrant(s) got to the stage. This is a definite plus to the show.

After all the awards, the thank-you's (always thank the tech crew, as well as the other workers) and the last-minute announcements, and the audience has departed to party, comes the dread...

Teardown

In many ways, this is the toughest part. The show is over, it's time to party, and there has to be enough folks to disconnect and pack the equipment, get the duct tape off the floor and other surfaces (venues are notoriously intolerant of the practice of leaving things duct taped), roll up the wires, and carry all this heavy and valuable equipment off to a safe place, or more likely several such, depending on its ownership. For this, the audience must be out of the way. Here is where the Concom can still get you.

Of late, there has been a growing tendency to have a dance just after the masquerade. Please ensure that if they think your sound tech is going to leave their equipment and/or themself there to provide dance music, that they have agreed to this in advance. Otherwise, you may have more difficulty getting a sound tech the next masquerade. The setups for the masquerade and a dance are usually different, and the equipment may have to be moved and reconnected. Plus, there should be an hour between the end of the masquerade and a dance, or there are going to be significant safety problems with equipment movement and potential dancers. Guess who will get the blame if something happens.

The equipment is packed, the tech crew is partying, the entrants' media and other stuff are back in the possession of the Masquerade Director. But all is not over. The rental equipment still has to be returned the next day (or two), and you can't assume that the person who rented it can necessarily return it. Check in advance. And the senior members of the tech crew should be at the post-mortem.

Sound

A much more detailed sound guide can be found in Craig Jones' treatise. But the general needs are: a quick, skilled sound tech, a set of equipment, and supplies such as tools, duct tape, wire, etc. Mostly, the tech will have these, but they will need replacement for usage. Mikes are usually rented/borrowed from the venue, because they are both subject to breakage and something techs are loath to bring to cons, except for the cheap variety. Sound setup is not as manpower intensive as lights, but will consume manpower and space. In general, the tech will need at least one helper, and access to the entry forms tech section. They will need access to these at least an hour before start time in order to make their notes on cuing and extract information from entrants who may not be really familiar with how to tell him what to do. Otherwise, they get the default.

Personnel selection is very important in sound - the requirements for masquerade sound are materially different from the DJ kind of sound. Avoid the "personality" type of tech. The important factors, other than technical competence, are calmness under fire, quickness in contestant media operations, and the ability to make do with available hardware under the budget restrictions of a con.

Getting the media cued is a very difficult thing, primarily because of misunderstanding by entrants of the timing of things, and the wish by the tech to make sure that the media is audible and yet not too loud. There is no overall satisfactory answer except for the entrants to bring their media to the masquerade pre-meeting/tech rehearsal/check in, and have the sound tech play the contestant media, calibrate the volume, and re-cue them with the entrant right there. This also allows them to make sure the correct side is being played, the media is identified rather than just the box it comes in, and bias and Dolby status known. Several of the sound techs have also redone media on the spot for people whose media were in poor condition, damaged, or nonexistent. Do not advertise this service unless the sound tech has agreed to it in advance, however.

The last call for the sound tech is to turn over the entrants' media to the Masquerade Director and to attend the post-mortem.

Lights

The lighting crew has perhaps the most difficult job of all in regards to coordination, timing, and complexity of effect. They will also consume most of the equipment budget, setup time and manpower, and have the greatest effect on spectacular costumes. The Lighting Head is usually the Tech Director, and is also usually the person most involved in the rental, storage, setup, teardown, and return of the equipment.

The usual lighting setup for a midsized masquerade involves two light trees, with eight to 16 ellipsoidals each, one or two follow-spots, gels for both the above, a dimmer pack, a lighting control board, and a lot of cable. These are almost always rented. The lighting head should be the person doing the rental and picking up the equipment, because the rental stuff has to be checked out prior to use, and they are likely the only one who will be able to do that. Also, power from the venue will be required (both 115VAC and 208 3-phase), and the Lighting Head is the most likely to engage in tech conversation with the venue engineer. All this implies that the Lighting Head needs to be a part of the team early on, at least four to six months before the con, and remain in close contact.

Lighting setup is complicated and full of pitfalls, from getting ladders to put up the light trees to connecting several dozen cables to color-balancing the ellipsoidals. Find the pro and let them do it. Someone with a little theater or college experience is most likely. Some of the personnel selection criteria are the same as the Sound Tech: calm, competent, flexible, quick, and non-ego bound.

Support is necessary, so if the selectee does not have a set of like-minded friends available, it is necessary to set up help in advance through the fannish network. The one sure way to kill a good lighting person is to leave them to do everything with no support, especially in the after-con period where a lot of techs end up having to do all equipment returns and clean up by themselves. So, a support staff should be included in the planning process, even though 90% of the time the tech has access to a group who will take this off your hands in return for a comp membership.

If the lighting tech has not done masquerades before, a training session will be necessary, preferably with recordings of past masquerades so they can see how it is done. This should be done before completely committing to this person, because they may come to their senses and another person-hunt will start.

The stage layout and lighting planning must be done at the time the final masquerade budget is being established. This is because they will have some determining effect on that budget. A room where, for traffic flow reasons, the power cables must be run on three sides to avoid crossing a doorway, will significantly add to the cable rental budget. A low ceiling will result in non-standard light trees. Difficult power outlets will increase adapter costs. Too few risers available from the venue will mean rental costs for those. Then, there is the issue of telling potential entrants about the setup so they can choreograph their presentations. One of the things they like to know is the tech layout so they can make use of the capabilities.

There are some circumstances where the budget is fat or equipment is available for other reasons where additional capabilities, such as floor lighting, or backlighting, or strobe lighting are available. This is an area of artistic judgement where, if the capability is there, people will use it whether or not it is enhancing or detracting from the costume. A good lighting person, with an experienced entrant, can generate a blow-away show. Unfortunately, the tendency of only not-quite-so-experienced entrants is to use all that capability because it is there. The result, in the graphic words of one tech, "looks like a dog's breakfast." In priority order, the floor/back strip is not a bad idea, but a strobe is rarely a good one, if just for the masquerade and not for a halftime show or something.

Video

The primary reasons for video are twofold: first, to provide a record of performances for archives and entrants' enjoyment, and second, to show the masquerade to groups, such as other entrants and people unable to get into the ballroom, who could not otherwise see it.

There is a consistent argument with conventions over compensation for the videos, with Concoms maintaining they should produce copies and sell them, and private individuals maintaining they should be able to either produce them and sell at cost to friends, or produce and sell at a profit (often with some nominal percentage to the con). This argument will go on forever. It will not be solved here, other than to note that the record of cons actually producing videos is abysmal, while the private guys actually put them out, and at a lower price.

The tech crew only has to be concerned with the technical arrangements for video, which usually involve a camera or cameras feeding a signal back to a monitor backstage for the entrants and/or to the venue cable distribution system and thence to the rooms. While there are some RF distribution systems which can eliminate cabling, 90% of the time this means running 75 ohm cable from a video site in front of the stage to the backstage monitor. A multicamera system will require a controller and cabling to/from the cameras, usually arranged one close and one far for pan view.

Early liaison with the venue will be necessary to use their cable system, although they are used to it and usually do not object. The venue engineer will need to talk with the video person and get such things as drive levels established. A channel assignment needs to be made, and published in convention literature.

Video cameras are still subject to a lot of reliability problems, so always have two available, even if only one is to be used. Since they are usually borrowed instead of rented, this is not a budget issue. Be careful to get the relatively new non-blooming solid-state ones, though, or the wildly varying light levels in the performances will make for a poor video. The equipment list is rounded out by one or two booster amplifiers, enough cable to reach the monitor and cable distribution point, a splitter, a monitor (preferably about 25 inches or so), tripod, extension cords (don't trust the batteries), and repair kit. Cables are really easy to break.

Personnel selection for this job is similar to sound and lights, but due to the reduced criticality and wider availability of experienced personnel, a bit more latitude is in order. Except for avoiding hysteria.

The same duct taping of cabling applies to video as to lights and sound. Safety is of primary importance.

TIPS ON VIDEO RECORDING MASQUERADES

By Rusty Dawe

The following article is reprinted from CostumApa 33. Its author, Rusty Dawe is the main man behind the camera and the professional editor for 3D Enterprises. He has been video head for a number of conventions and has produced beautifully edited, multi-camera video tapes for Costume Cons 5, 6, 7, & 8, plus Westercons 38, 39 & 40 as well as many others.

By now I must have viewed more masquerades as seen from more different angles than just about anyone (with the possible exceptions of Carl Mami and John Fong). The following list of DOs and DON'Ts are distilled from the many, MANY hours of editing masquerade video and wishing that camera "A" would have stayed on costume "'N" just a little longer, or that camera "B" would not have jerked at just that same instant (sigh).

Having also been behind the camera and trying to practice what I know are proper techniques, I also understand why many of these techniques are not self-evident or necessarily easy to implement After all. it is fairly easy to critique camera work while sitting back in the relative solitude of the editing lab and quite a different thing to coherently follow one of Animal X's madcap presentations when it is happening live in front of you and this is the first time anyone has ever seen it… Case in point, Animal X's presentation of "Princess Kawyt-Tisi" at Costume-Con 6 was the only presentation in all three masquerades that required shots from all five cameras we had running, and I still didn't always have an angle I really wanted to use!

This list applies to all situations, regardless of camera position or number of cameras that you are working with. Where applicable, I will mention appropriate actions (if different) when one is taping with a multiple camera operation.

> *Masquerades are "live" and usually unrehearsed. It is a challenge to out- guess what the costumer will do. Sometimes you'll even guess right!*

#1- **Move the camera s-l-o-w-1-y** and smoothly. This is without a doubt the single most important point to remember for getting good quality footage with your camera.

Although it sounds simple enough, this is also probably one of the most difficult points to master, especially during taping of a masquerade. This is because there is often too much happening too quickly to take in without radical camera motion. The following will help you achieve calm camera motion under the most demanding situations

- Use a tripod. This is a must for taping a masquerade. You just can't hold the camera steady enough for long enough.

- Don't tighten your tripod too tight. This is a typical cause of jerkiness.

  Both horizontal and vertical motion should be possible at both slow and fast speeds without the tripod locking the motion. The adjustments should be loose enough that the camera would probably tilt forward or backward on its own accord if you weren't there to steady it Of course if you are going to walk away from the camera. go ahead and tighten it up.

- Start all camera motions slowly and then build up speed only after you are already on the move (i.e. try to keep a constant acceleration/deceleration until you reach the top speed you are willing to move the camera at).

- Note that if you are farther away and zoomed in close that it takes less physical motion of the camera to travel the same effective distance in the lens (vs. being close with the lens wide).

- The top speed is NOT a fast speed. It is better to miss a little action by moving the camera slowly than to capture it and make your viewers all seasick!

- Limit the number of required camera motions. You can do this by widening your lens if possible, to take in more of the action. Close ups are nice, but worthless if you are continuously chasing your target around the stage! Another option is to skip taping some of the action. This is anathema to many who record masquerades but is often necessary (this is why multiple camera editing is important!). This is discussed more in item #2-groups, and item #4, below.

#2 - Frame your subject. How much is enough? How close is too close? This is another point which sounds easy to do but requires a little thought to pull off and make "invisible" to your viewing audience. Under all conditions, you want to fill your lens as much as possible Don't let a costume end up looking like an ant in a desert by pulling so far back as to see this little dinky person lost among all that huge stage. Try to keep zoomed in as close as possible without requiring excessive camera motion. The following will help you frame your subject under a variety of conditions.

- The single costume: Although everyone wants to see "all" of a costume, 90% of the time framing just the head and torso of a single subject in the lens will give you the best results. It turns out that most people watch other people's faces when they talk to each other and this carries over into the way they view TV and movies. So, by concentrating your camera on the upper body of your subject, you will present your viewers with the level of detail they are most comfortable observing.

A good technique to give the viewer both the full body view and the close-up of the head/torso is to start with the full body and then if the subject starts to walk toward you, don't pull back on the zoom until the subject fills the lens with the upper body. Then follow the subject smoothly with the zoom as they continue to walk toward you in order to keep the size of the subject constant

- The pair which separates: This is a typical tricky situation which you will run into over and over while taping a masquerade. There are two choices here.

  1) Keep pulling back to try to keep both costumes in view.

  2) Choose one of the two costumes and follow it, ignoring the other costume.

Unfortunately, many people chose a third option - track both costumes as far as they can then switch to one, then to the other, then back to the first, and so forth. Generally, you want to option (2). Unless the two costumes are doing a presentation which will not read unless both costumes are viewed together, you will find that ignoring one of them for part of your taping will allow you to concentrate on the other to best advantage.

I have found that when the two costumes split, back up a little to keep both in view for just a bit, then follow the costume which is coming toward you and treat it as a single costume (i.e. you now have a good view of the front of at least one of the costumes, so get a good shot of it - the other costume probably had their back to you anyway!

- The large group: This is the single camera operator's nemesis. There is just too much going on to track with a single camera, so just get it straight in your mind that you won't get it all and you will be ahead of the game from the start. If you are far enough back to get all the action in your lens, you should stay at this distance for at least part of the presentation to get an overall feel for all of the costumes (again, be sure that you frame the costumes and not the stage). However, if you stay back for the entire presentation, you won't really see any of the costumes well. This is where you will have to be discriminating.

After taping the entire group for a bit, pick out one or two costumes worth zooming in on and follow them, ignoring the rest (ignoring some of the action is the hardest pan of taping a group). Pick costumes which are facing you and which you can treat as a single or pair. Usually at the end of group presentations, all the costumes exit the same way, so you usually have a chance to get a close up of them one at a time when they leave. More in item #4, below

#3 - Limit use of the zoom: This is important for the same reasons as stated for moving the camera. You can tell you are overusing the zoom capability of your camera if you feel like you are always left wanting more of a given costume subject and yet it is within the viewing area much of the time. This is the effect of not permitting the subject to present itself without a change of perspective or viewing position. Of course, this is assuming that the camera was not moving radically at the same time - a far more obvious problem. The following may help reduce your use of the zoom.

- Pull back a little so that you don't have to re-adjust as often. If you find you are constantly changing the zoom to keep the subject properly framed as was suggested in item #2, above, you are probably too close overall. Back off just a little bit and don't try to get in as close as often.

- Use the motion of your subject to change your zoom distance for you! This works really great if you are filming subjects which are walking toward or away from you. Often you will be able to get that close up shot without actually moving the zoom at all. Your subject will just walk right into your frame. This works best if you know in advance what the costumer will do, but foreknowledge is not required. Many masquerades have a standard runway pattern and after the first couple of costumes you will probably know in advance where most of the costumes will enter and exit

#4 - Edit your subject: We have already touched on this point a little when discussing large group costumes, but even when nothing appears to be going on, you have some choices as to what to record; i.e. do you record a blank stage or the MC picking their nose? In general action (any action) is preferable to a blank stage. I tend to keep with the MC until just before the next costume comes out then shift to the stage entrance. Often, if you have positioned your camera correctly. the stage entrance and MC will be in the lens at the same time, so that you can

focus on the MC, then follow the costumes out when they appear on stage behind them or over the MC's shoulder (usually with just a minor change in the zoom). Also, at the end of a presentation, following the costumes until they are out of sight or make a transition out of the lighted stage area is preferable to cutting back quickly to the MC as soon as the costume begins to exit the stage. Occasionally you will catch a look or expression on the face of the costumer that is priceless as they realize they are done and still alive!

What do you record when there is too much going on to follow coherently? Actually, most of the time it sorts itself out for you. You want your record to look as good as you can and show off the costumes you are taping to the best advantage. The following list of taping priorities may help you decide which action to follow when it is all coming apart at the seams...

1) Pick the center-piece costume. Often you will have a group of costumes of which most are support costumes to a main one. Concentrate your camera work on the main costume and track the peripheral costumes only when you can't get a good angle on the main costume or it is turned away from you.

2) Try to pick a spot on the stage through which all the costumes are moving. Some presentations will crisscross all the costumes or march everyone through a circle or similar pattern. By finding a spot which all the costumes pass through, you can catch all the action and never have to move the camera once. This looks great when it works, but isn't always obvious at first.

3) Pick the costume or costumes which are directly facing you or coming toward you.

4) Pick costumes which are moving in a predictable manner. Ignore action which is changing abruptly and which will be gone by the time you get it in focus.

5) All other conditions being equal and your camera position is off center, you should aim at the side opposite from you. You will find it easier to follow the action when it is farther from you than when it is twisting and turning right under your nose.

6) Give up and pull all the way back. Sometimes you just have to say "What the F-."

#5 - Camera Placement: When setting up your camera prior to the masquerade, you often have a choice of where to set up. If you are a single camera, your best choices are:

1) About 20 feet back from stage on the side opposite the MC and masquerade entrance (usually the far right side of the audience). This way you have a clear shot at the masquerade contestants as they enter and can follow them off stage until they are well into the audience. Due to the effect of the camera on those sitting behind you, you will usually find yourself behind the audience against the side wall in order to obtain this angle. This is not bad and often preferable to having people tripping over your tripod.

2) Center back. If the masquerade tech crew provides a riser at the center back (usually at the end of a runway that contestants walk down), this is an excellent spot Even if you don't have a riser, you can often obtain a good angle by positioning the camera on the aisle near the rear if there is a large center aisle.

3) Half way back on the side to all the way back on the side. If you have a good telephoto lens this isn't as bad as it might seem. It is easier to get an overall feel for larger presentations from here than it is from up close and you can usually follow the costumes across stage pretty easily.

4) Down in front (close to stage). This is a really tough spot. While you may be able to get some really great close-ups, overall, you will have a tough time following the costumes and keeping the camera from whipping continually from side to side across the stage. Also, when the angle gets extreme you can often find yourself staring directly into the stage lighting. This location is best if you are doing a two camera edit. That way the front camera can obtain the close-ups while the back camera can cover the overall action.

5) Photo area. While you miss all of the presentations from here, you get outstanding detail shots of all the costumes under decent lighting. If doing a multi-camera edit, this location is a must! If the main masquerade hall is dimly lit and there is a good available-light photo area set up, you should give serious consideration to this location.

Well, I think this is enough on this subject for now. I may add some additional points in the future (probably while editing another masquerade to give vent to my frustrations!). I hope you find these tips of use. Good shooting!

MASQUERADE AUDIO HANDBOOK
- COSTUMER'S VERSION

By Craig L. Jones
Second Edition, 17 January 1988

Table of Contents

There is also a supplement to this handbook intended for those who are in charge of running the masquerade event.

About the Author

Craig Jones, a computer consultant by day, has been working as an audio/visual technician on the side for over a decade. His theater production credits include Sound Designer, Stage Manager, Audio Technician, and Lighting Technician, and he has been in charge of the audio/visual division of several conventions. In addition, Mr. Jones has produced two documentary multi-media shows, been the editor of two newsletters, and is a published author of non-fiction articles. He is currently writing his first science fiction novel.

Over the last six years Mr. Jones has been developing a special interest in the production of costume contests, particularly in the area of sound. He has collected and cross-referenced a variety of music and sound effects and organized it in such a way that most of the material can be accessed at literally a moment's notice.

At the costume contest held during Phantasmicon IV, he was able to provide from his portable library a suitable soundtrack for all but one of the 50 some odd entries. For the LA Con II World SF Convention, however, he wasn't satisfied with merely providing "canned generics" and set up a small recording studio in a hotel meeting room. In the three and a half days leading up to the masquerade event, he recorded and mixed down 28 of the 109 tapes that were used.

1 - Introduction

1.1 - How to Read this Handbook. It was my intent to write the body of this document in such a manner that you could either read it straight through or skip around at will. This meant that each section had to be completely self-sufficient and not assume familiarity with other sections; yet, the document as a whole could not be redundantly redundant. My solution was to create an extensive glossary which appears in an appendix at the end.

If a word or phrase appears in italics, then it is listed in the glossary. The first time you encounter such a word, you might need to look it up, but thereafter, you will know its meaning and not be subjected to it again and again.

1.2 - Intended Readership. This handbook is for EVERYONE who participates in costume masquerades in any way shape or form (except maybe being in the audience). Whether you are putting together a soundtrack or just rehearsing with it, running the sound for an event or just helping to set up chairs, you'll find information in this handbook that ought to be useful. (Note: A supplement that accompanies this handbook will be of interest to those of you who are in charge of running the sound for an event.)

For example, if you are a member of a group that is entering the contest, you'll know that your recording engineer will make several copies of your soundtrack (one to turn in, one for a back-up, and one or more to rehearse with) and you'll know not to get them confused. Or, let's say you're assisting the Masquerade Director to set up the hall. When the audio technician asks you to set up the sound table in what appears to be the best seat in the house, you'll know they are not being vain, but rather that they must be able to hear what the audience hears or else what the audience hears won't be any good.

2 - Basic Recording and Editing Techniques

Many fancy recording techniques have been devised over the years to facilitate the creation of numerous audio effects; however, it only takes three basic techniques, *mixing*, *splicing*, and *multi-track recording*, to handle the preparation of most masquerade recordings.

2.1 – Mixing. A mixing console, or mixer, allows two or more channels of audio signal to be combined into one. Basic mixers allow for different volume levels to be set for each input signal. A good mixer will also provide tone control (*equalization*), input padding to switch between microphone and *line-level* inputs, and pan pots to balance the input between the left and right outputs. (Please don't worry if you did not follow all of what I just said.) In a live situation a mixer could be used to take any number of microphones and instrument pick-ups and mix them down to be fed into the two inputs (left and right) of an amplifier. In a recording studio, the signals could come from any number of devices besides microphones such as turntables, tape decks, reverb tanks, etc.

Mixers are not commonly found in home stereo systems, and I don't recommend going out and buying one just to make masquerade tapes; however, you might already have (or easily acquire) a tape recorder with a "sing along" feature. This is where the tape deck will record what is coming in from both the line-level and microphone inputs at the same time. If your tape deck has this feature, you will want to experiment with it to see how the various controls affect the volume levels of the inputs (if at all).

2.2 – Splicing. This is the action of piecing together different sounds, one right after another, into one cohesive program. In the old days, it was accomplished physically with a razor blade and adhesive splicing tape on a reel-to-reel tape deck. These days, it's all done in software.

2.3 - Multi-track Recording. This is a recording technique where different channels worth of audio -- which will eventually be mixed together -- are first recorded onto different tracks of an intermediate tape. This gives the recording technician room for error. If in the final mix, they don't get the right combination of levels, they can mix it again without having to re-record everything from scratch. Again, in the old days this was done on a multi-track reel-to-reel tape deck, but these days it's all digital.

2.4 - An Example Using All Three Techniques.

Step 1: Write a script. The initial phase of any project, be it creating a soundtrack or a building a house, is to do a *requirements analysis*. A builder can't just jump right in and pour the foundation until they know how big the house will be. Likewise, before you even touch your recording equipment, you should invest a little time in determining ALL of your needs. Think about such things as the timing of your presentation, the mood you are trying to set, any information you are trying to get across, and any aspects of your presentation that you would like to be highlighted.

Let us suppose you've been having fun with Friendly Plastic lately and have built half a dozen mutant costumes for you and your friends. After hearing about the nuclear accident at the Chernobyl power plant, you realize that you'd like to make a statement with your costumes by setting your presentation to Sting's song "I Hope the Russians Love Their Children Too."

So, you go out and buy the recording. You listen to it several times and note down such things as how long the introduction is, how far into the song you can cut it (fade it out), and how appropriate the words really are. Then you write your script. You figure that the song speaks for itself, so you don't need to add any narration, but you also note that while the tone of the music is plenty sad, it doesn't convey enough shock. Additionally, knowing what limited mobility the costumes offer, you wish that the introduction was eight to ten seconds longer.

You figure out that you can solve both problems at once by first recording eight seconds worth of military sound effects (air raid siren, bombings, etc.), and then *cross-fading* into the music. So far, your script looks like this:

:00 Start sound effects (air raid siren, people running, gunfire and bombings). Human female wearing gas mask enters from *stage right* and runs to the bomb shelter (only the door of which is seen at the *stage left* end of the stage.) She closes the door and locks it just as two more humans appear stage right. (They are wearing mutant costumes under their normal (loose) clothing and they are also wearing gas masks.) They pound on the door, but no one lets them in.

:05 Sound of one big (nuclear) explosion. Couple still pounding on door react to blast by falling to stage floor apparently knocked unconscious. Their clothing tears as they fall (Velcro).

:08 Sound effects end as music *fades in*. Woman emerges from bomb shelter, coughing and wheezing with a handkerchief over her face. She sees the fallen couple and bends down to help them, removing the mask from the nearest one. She is at once appalled by the mutant's deformities and shrinks back into the shelter.

:15 Three more mutants enter and attack the two unconscious ones. (The second gas mask comes off in the struggle.) As the two wake up to defend themselves, they manage to fend off the attackers long enough to begin attacking the door to the shelter. The other three see what the two are doing and join in.

:25 The mutants are able to pull the door from its hinges and fling it aside. They go in and forcibly remove the woman along with her husband and son. The mutants kill the father and the boy, and then three of them drag the woman off kicking and screaming (exit stage right). The remaining two mutants drag the corpses off in the same direction.

:30 Music is faded out after the second chorus.

Step 2: Initial rehearsals. Even though you realize that it might be difficult to get the masquerade crew to provide appropriately dramatic lighting effects, you decide that the presentation will still work well enough in constant light, so you proceed with your plans; however, before you bother to make the actual show tape (with the sound effects added to the music and the music faded out at the right place), you call for initial rehearsals to begin.

For these run throughs you utilize a scratch tape -- one with just the music which cuts out abruptly after 30 seconds, and you get someone with a stopwatch to fake the sound effects by banging on a table and so forth. After three or four rehearsals, you realize that your estimated timing was a little off. What you really need is 15 seconds of sound effects at the beginning and you need to fade out the music before the second chorus rather than after. Now, finally, you are ready to work on the actual show tape.

Step 3: Creating the show recording. The first thing you should do is plan the logistics of how you will be able to go from raw materials to final product. Think it through from beginning to end.

(Note: The following refers to using old-school equipment such as tape decks and record turntables, but the same overall concepts apply to digital techniques. Software just makes it much easier.)

Can you process both the record with military sounds and the record with the nuclear explosion simultaneously, or do you have to transfer one of them to tape first because you only have one turntable? Do you need to worry about fading one channel up or down while another stays constant, or can you get away with a *Y-adapter* because at the critical point one piece fades naturally? Do you have enough hands to work all of the controls or do you need to enlist the aid of a helper?

In this case, let's suppose that you have at your disposal a stereo system with a turntable and a tape deck, and you are able to borrow a second tape deck to hook into it. You have two records. One is a sound effects record that has the miscellaneous military sounds on one band and the nuclear explosion on another. The second record is the Sting album. Because you only have one turntable and because the two sound effects are on the same record, the plan is to first transfer the nuclear explosion effect to tape. To do this requires no modification to how your stereo is already set up. You simply copy the record to tape. (Using both channels is fine at this point).

Now for the tricky part. The patch cords between the receiver and the primary tape deck (the one used to record the nuclear explosion) need to be removed and replaced with a Y-adapter that combines both outputs from the receiver into one input on the tape deck (say the left channel). Next, the secondary tape deck needs to be wired up with both of its outputs connected through a Y-adapter to the other (right) input of the primary tape deck. Take the tape with the nuclear explosion out of the primary tape deck and put in the secondary tape deck. (Cue it back to the beginning.) Put a blank tape in the primary deck so that it can be used to record the combined soundtrack. The system is now set up so that material from the turntable (e.g. the military sounds and the music) can be recorded onto one track of the fresh tape while the explosion can be re-recorded onto the other track (as shown):

```
R: (noises)                              ---- explosion ----   (noises) -->
L: (noises)    ---- military sounds ----  (noises)        ---- music ----->
```

Now, with the explosion cued up (that is, with the secondary tape deck in play mode but paused) start the primary tape deck recording and then start playing the military sounds on the turntable. At the appropriate point, de-pause the secondary tape deck to start the explosion and then quickly stop the turntable and remove the sound effects record. Replace it with the Sting album. (Don't worry if noises from picking up the needle get recorded as they won't wind up on the final tape.) After the explosion has gone on long enough (the time it takes to switch records is probably plenty), start the turntable back up and place the needle down in front of the song ("I Hope the Russians... "). Let the explosion keep going well after the music has started until it is at the point at which you are sure the explosion should have been completely faded out. The actual fading will be done later. Likewise, let the music keep going until after the second chorus (even though you plan to fade it out before that).

The last step is what is known as the final mixdown. The connections will have to rearrange again, this time so that instead of the outputs from the secondary tape deck (both channels) only going into the right channel of the primary deck, they are fed into both of its channels. To accomplish this, disconnect the Y-adapter from between the receiver and the primary deck's left input and turn it around, inserting it between the other Y-adapter and the two inputs of the primary deck.

(You will need a gender-changing adapter to connect the two Y-adapters together.) Essentially, you will have hooked the two tape decks together via an "X-adapter."

```
Secondary   Left Output :  -------.        .------ : Left Input    Primary
   Tape                              |---|                          Tape
   Deck    Right Output :  ------ '        `------ : Right Input    Deck
```

Now, move the tape that is currently in the primary deck to the secondary deck and put a fresh (third) tape in the primary deck. (Do not re-use the tape with the explosion in case something went wrong with recording the second tape, so that at least you won't have to start completely from scratch.) To do the mixdown, simply copy the tape in the secondary deck to the new tape in the primary deck and adjust the volume levels as you go (fading in and out when appropriate). These adjustments have to be done by changing the output volume levels on the secondary tape deck (i.e. before they get mixed together via the Y-adapters). Note: some tape decks do not have independent output volume level controls (or even any at all); however, in order for this scheme to work (as described here), the secondary tape deck must have such controls. See Additional recording techniques below for alternative mix-down schemes.

You now have your final show tape (still in the primary tape deck). To make additional copies of it you can either repeat the mixdown process with fresh tapes, or you can move this first copy to the secondary tape deck and copy it straight across.

Step 4: Dress rehearsals. By not assuming that the tape would come out exactly the way you had in mind, you were sure to schedule a couple of dress rehearsals. Not only does this allow you to see the whole presentation come together, but it also gives the cast an opportunity to practice listening for their cues.

In this case, you quickly and unfortunately find out that the limited mobility of the costumes is an even worse problem than you imagined, and try as you might, you can't get the cast to get the timing down at all. Finally, when it gets to the point where everyone can't stop laughing, you decide to scrap the whole nuclear accident idea and make a soundtrack out of Weird Al Yankovich's' "Slime Creatures From Outer Space" instead.

3 - Additional Recording Techniques

3.1 - Microphone Placement. When using a hand-held microphone, it is best to hold it so that when you talk, your breath goes across the top of the mike rather than directly into it. For one thing, breathing into some microphones can cause damage. (Never blow into a microphone to see if it is on -- tap it with your fingertips instead.) Such placement also has the advantage of avoiding loud "P-pops," and (if you are on stage) allows the audience to see your smile.

3.2 - Setting the Recording Level. Most tape recorders have VU (volume unit) meters to show you the intensity of the signal that is being recorded (on each track). The best recordings are when the needle (or LED lights) are riding as high as they can without going into the red. (It is okay if it goes into the red occasionally, say up to 5 or 10 times a minute.) When it does go into the red, the recording will be (slightly) distorted because the tape can't handle it. (If you put 4 cubic feet of clothes in a 3 cubic foot suit case, they're going to come out wrinkled.) On the other hand, you don't want the recording levels to be too soft either since you want the biggest possible difference between the signal and the noise which is inherent in any recording. (This is known as the *signal to noise ratio.*)

3.3 - Converting Stereo to Mono. This can be done in several ways. Some stereo systems have mono buttons built into them so that when depressed, they cause the two input channels to be combined with the result being sent equally to both outputs. (Warning, this feature might mono the output going to the speakers, but still send stereo to the tape deck.)

A second method is to go through a mixer, This has the advantage that you can control the relative volume levels of the two input channels. (Note: This advantage is usually only needed if the two inputs are altogether different as opposed to being the left and right channels of a stereo recording.)

The third, and simplest/cheapest method is the utilization of a *Y-adapter*. This is a special patch cord that can connect the two output feeds of, say, your stereo system into one of the line level inputs of your tape deck. Y-adapters can be purchased practically anywhere that stereos are sold, If you are not sure what you need, bring with you the patch cord(s) that connect your stereo to the tape deck normally to show the salesman what kind of connectors they use. (WARNING! Do not use a Y-adapter between your turntable and its input to the stereo. If you want to combine the signals coming from the record, do so after they go through the stereo system (i.e. after going through a *pre-amp*) and before going into the tape recorder.

3.4 - Alternate Mix-Down Techniques. As I said, the mix-down setup described in section 2.4 using two tape decks hooked together with two Y-adapters (forming one X-adapter) requires that the deck being used for playback has an independent playback volume control for each channel. If you can't find such a tape deck, then there are two alternatives. The first is straight-forward but expensive: use a genuine mixer in place of the two Y-adapters. Can't afford that? Then try the following alternative which is a little more complicated but free:

First, hook up the two tape decks as you normally would in order to duplicate tapes using two straight-through patch cords connecting the left channel of one deck to the left channel of the other deck. Likewise, connect right to right, Now, using the recording level controls on the primary tape deck (which is doing the recording) instead of the playback controls on the secondary tape deck (which don't exist), do the mix-down as described in 2. 4, fading in and out as appropriate.

Never mind the fact that some parts of your soundtrack will only be copied onto the right channel and other parts onto the left (for now). You may want to try it three or four times until you get the mix-down just right, but be sure to use a different blank tape for each attempt just in case your first attempt turns out to be the best one anyway.

Once you have a mixdown made to your satisfaction, all that remains is to make one final copy of it with the two channels unified. To do this you will need to hook up the two tape decks with the now infamous X-adapter (2 Y-adapters). Place the good mix-down tape into the secondary tape deck (the playback deck) and place yet another blank tape into the primary deck, Now, just make a copy of the mix-down tape. Because of the two Y-adapters, the copy will get both channels of the mix down tape combined onto each of its two channels.

4 - Media Standards

The following are the guidelines that I use when making up final show media. At least, this is how I like to see the media when I am the audio tech for the event. You will certainly want to see if the audio tech for the contest you are entering has a different opinion.

4..1 - Labeling Media. The upper half of the label should list the name of the entry and the real name of one person in the group. (Use the same name on all paperwork.) If the name of the entry is not descriptive, then you might add in parenthesis a one-word description such as "warrior," "clowns," or "princess," so the audio tech will know what he's looking for. (Note: be sure to leave about a half-inch square in the upper-left corner of the label for the tech (not you) to write in your entry number.

The lower half of the label should contain the total running time of the soundtrack in minutes and seconds (e.g. "2:34") and a description of the type(a) of sounds contained in the soundtrack. Please limit such descriptions to the following vocabulary: "music,", "voice," "effects," "and" (or a plus sign), and "then." For example, if your soundtrack consists of music with a voice-overdub that begins 15 seconds into the piece, then describe it as "music then music + voice."

For cassette tapes, the label on the back side should either be completely blank or, preferably, contain only the phrase "wrong side." Now, I've heard it told that on at least one occasion the audio technician played the wrong side despite it being labeled. I don't know if this is true, but I guess it wouldn't be a bad idea to record your soundtrack on both sides of the tape, just in case; HOWEVER, if you do, you should still label one side as wrong. Otherwise, you'll confuse the hell out of the technician and that is the last thing you want to do.

Note: Use a dark color ink (black falls in this category, yellow does not) on a pale color label (white is a good choice here). If the cassette you bought didn't come with a label or has a label that is too dark or busy, then cover it with a white file folder label that you can buy at any stationary store. Cover the back side as well.

4.2 – Choosing a Tape. *(This is old-school advice, of course.)* Cassette tapes come in four grades: metal, chrome (high bias), normal bias, and trash.

The latter is the kind they sell in three packs at the drug store. All you have to do is look at them funny for them to jam up or break on you, and, of course, they always wait until the exact wrong time do it.

Now, this ·doesn't mean you should over-compensate and spend six dollars on a metal tape either. That would just be a waste of money. Personally, I don't even use chrome (70μs). I find that normal bias tapes (120μs) work just fine, and since that is what most contestants turn in anyway, I make it easy on myself and go that route too. At least, that way I avoid constantly changing the bias settings on the playback tape decks during the event.

One more thing: the longer a tape is, the thinner is has to be to fit in the cassette. And the thinner a tape is, the higher the chance of it stretching or breaking. For this reason, I never use 120 minute tapes and I don't even trust putting 90 minute tapes in the player in my car. As far as show tapes go, I am currently using Fuji 46 minute tapes that I found on sale for 76 cents each. Before that I was using 10 and 20 minute cassettes that I bought in bulk for 70 cents each, which were filled with TDK brand tape. It really doesn't matter. Practically any name brand tape up to size C-60 will do. (TDK, Fuji, Maxell, BASF, Sony, etc.)

4.3 - Not Using Dolby. For the same reason that I don't use chrome or metal tapes, I don't use Dolby or any other kind of noise reduction when I make up show tapes. Most contestants do not have Dolby, or bother to use it if they do, and I go along with it.

4.4 -Skipping the Leader. When using tape, no matter what you write on the label or tell the audio tech ahead of time, I can almost guarantee you that they (or more likely an assistant) will rewind your tape and then advance it past the leader before the show starts. So, if you turn in a pre-recorded tape that is cued to the beginning of the third song on side B, what you're going to get is the first song on side A. (Also, in for a surprise is any contestant who times their routine to include the five second leader at the start of the tape.) Dealing with the case of the pre-recorded tape is simply a matter of finding a friend with two tape decks, and having them copy just the song you want onto a fresh tape at the beginning of side A.

Solving the problem of needing time to set up is a little trickier. You could just include the pause you need on the tape after the end of the leader; however, when the audio tech doesn't hear anything, he'll think there is something wrong. Probably the best thing to do is to first record some sound effect right after the leader -- wind chimes, a lion roar, anything that will set the mood - then leave your blank stretch, and then start your music (or whatever). This also has the advantage that when you hear your sound effect, you know it is your cue to start.

4.5 - Turning in Your Media. Unfortunately, there is no standard that specifies when contestants are to turn in their tapes or other media. When I am the audio tech I like to get them turned in as early as possible (i.e. at the time of registration) so that I can review them, but I've seen other technicians who would rather not take a chance on losing them and don't want to see them until the contestants line up.

So, my suggestion is that you be prepared for both, and I mean BOTH. Make at least two copies of your media. Bring one with you when you register and ask the registrar if they want it at that time. (Don't force it upon them.) Then, even if they take it, bring the second copy to the line-up. (You never know when there might be a foul up in communications which results in the media not getting from the registrar to the audio tech.)

Be sure that both copies of your media are labeled exactly the same. (Oh, all right. You can add the words "Duplicate Copy" to the second one if you wish.) Just don't confuse the audio tech should they happen to wind up with both of them by, for example, labeling one copy with only the title of your entry and labeling the other with only your name.

4.6 - Cuing Playback. Unless told otherwise, (maybe even then) the audio technician will start playing your media at the first sign of your group entering or when the MC starts their introduction, AND NOT BEFORE. If it is possible to plan your presentation to coincide with this practice, then do so; otherwise, contact the Masquerade Director about making an exception, and then plan a contingency for when your request is ignored or forgotten anyway.

5 - Dos and Don'ts

In a nutshell, the two rules to remember are to cover your ass, and don't get fancy. These words of wisdom are plain enough if you remember that the audio tech who will be playing your media is really a chimpanzee with an audio system. Actually, you can get as fancy as you like, but just don't deviate from the standards (see chapter 4), or do the unexpected. Yes, I know this puts a crimp on your style, but you can't blow away the audience if the audio tech screws it up for you. Consider:

Don't Use a Gradual Lead-in. If your soundtrack starts off quiet as a whisper and gradually fades in, you can be assured that the tech will panic when they don't hear anything at first. They will undoubtedly stop the playback and pull the media out of the player to see if they have it in the right way. Then, when that possibility doesn't pan out, they'll assume there is something wrong with the media and just not play it at all.

Do Bring Several Copies of Your Media. I've never seen media get lost between the time it was turned in to registration and the time it is supposed to show up at the sound table, but there is always a first. And then there's the possibility of the label falling off or the media getting mis-numbered, or recorded over, or bulk erased, or...

Do Bring Contingency Media. What is the likelihood of another contestant wanting to use the same music as you? If your costume is from a popular or recent TV show or movie, then it is probably pretty high, and you would be wise to bring not only the main theme song, but another part of the score, or even some completely different yet appropriate music as well.

Do Make Sure that the Audio Technician can Read the Label of Your Media. Print or type the information legibly with dark ink on a white label.

Don't Expect the Audio Technician to Read It. Just because you write special instructions on the label (which you shouldn't do) is no guarantee that the technician will notice them, much less be able to obey them.

Don't Blow into Any Microphone. Unless you know for a fact that doing so won't hurt it. See section 3.1.

Don't Attach a Y-adapter Directly to a Turntable. See section 3.3.

A - Suggested Sources for Material

A.1 - Music Stores.
- *Movie Soundtracks*: not only for recognizable theme songs but for non-recognizable instrumental score music that might go well with a presentation having nothing to do with the film.
- *Sound Effects*: Many Halloween sound effects records have "Halloween in outer space" effects. Check the children's section, too.
- *Classical Music*: Need I say more?
- *Popular Music*: Good for pieces based on current events and humorous bits.
- *Traditional/Folk Music*: Find them in with the classical.

A.2 - Public Library. Usually their records are terribly scratched, but cassette tapes and CDs are worth a listen.

A.3 - Television/Radio/Internet. Why not?

A.4 - Real Life. Try getting what you need by recording such things as machines & gadgets, video arcade games, people, etc. Be sure and play it for someone who is not involved in your group to see if s/he can tell what it is without any clues.

A.5 - Past Masquerade Events. Keep all of your media from past events in case you ever decide to re-create a presentation for some special occasion. Likewise, keep accurate notes on where the bits and pieces came from in case you ever decide to use a particular element again in a new soundtrack.

B - Alternatives to Narrating

The two most common approaches for scripting presentations have always been to (a) record a monologue and then lip-sync it, or (b) have a narrator describe the costume/character. They were great techniques when nobody else was doing them, but now everybody does them, and they have become boring. (Not to mention, lip synching is hard to do and looks funny if it isn't done perfectly.) So, I offer some alternatives:

B.1 - Personify the Spot Light(s). One of the tapes I made for LA Con II was for Princess Aura from the 1980 film *Flash Gordon*. She lip synched a few short lines, pleading with an unseen Ming the Merciless, "Please don't kill him yet, father. I want him. Give him to me." The omnipresent voice of Ming answers, "Really, Aura. Your appetites are too dangerous. I refuse!" All the while Aura's focus places the voice as emanating from the follow spot, above and behind the audience.

B.2 - Give the Narrator Some Character. If you have to use a narrator, then at least breathe some life into them. Say, for example, you have the best Star Trek uniform this side of Andromeda. Why not show it off by having Captain Kirk make an announcement on the ship's public address system about a surprise inspection while you fumble around on stage trying to find a hiding place for your 3-D centerfold magazine? A similar idea would be to have a Howard Cosell of the future give the play-by-play at the Galactic Olympics. Whatever your costume, it shouldn't be hard, with a little imagination, to create a soundtrack that will demonstrate your handiwork to the audience without lecturing them about it.

C - Where to Seek Help

C.1 - Local College. The theater arts department of your nearby college will likely have a faculty or staff member who will be happy to assist you. Some schools even have programs for recording engineers where you might find a student who is willing to get personally involved with your group.

C.2 - Community Theater Group. Likewise.

C.3 - High Fidelity Audio Store. The salesmen at audio specialty stores are usually knowledgeable about all types of equipment. If you are having trouble getting your equipment to work, bring it in and ask them about it. (Be sure to call first.) Sometimes all you need is simple adapter or patch cord which they can probably sell you. (It might be a little more expensive than at a discount store, but at least you'll know you are getting the right part.)

D - Bibliography

Eargle, John; *Sound Recording*; New York: Van Nostrand Reinhold Company, © 1980.

Kennedy, Peggy; *The Kennedy Masquerade Compendium*; Firepearl Editions, 7 North Lyons Avenue; Menands, New York 12204, © 1984.

Stern, Lawrence; *Stage Management: A Guidebook of Practical Techniques*. Massachusetts: Allyn and Bacon, Inc., © 1982.

Radio Magazine; March 1984; "Sound Reinforcement for the Amateur."

E - Glossary

auxiliary in - *See line in.*

band - An individual song or sound effect on a given side of a record. (E.g. the third song on the second side of an album might be referred to as "side B, band 3.")

channel - A single element of sound as processed by the audio equipment. For example, a stereo amplifier processes the audio program via two channels, left and right. A mixer that is capable of separately handling six inputs (e.g. from six microphones) is called a six-channel mixer. A tape deck that can record on four tracks at once would have inputs and outputs for four associated channels.

cross-fading - A *splicing* technique where the second piece of music (or whatever) begins *fading* in before the first piece is completely faded out, thus making a smooth transition. This is more difficult to pull off than other splicing techniques since it requires that both pieces along with appropriate equipment to play them on are available simultaneously, and that a mixer is available that can handle the cross-fade.

dubbing - A form of multi-track recording where instead of all of the tracks being recorded at once, they are recorded one at a time. (Note: This requires the use of a tape deck that can independently select tracks for recording.) An example of this might be where you first record some instrumental music on one track, say the left channel, and then go back and record a vocal track "on top of it" (i.e. on the right channel). Beware that you might have problems with timing if the tape deck has separate record and playback heads.

equalization - Adjusting the tone of the sound.

fading - A splicing technique where a piece of music (or some other audio program) is started or stopped by gradually turning the volume up or down rather than cutting it abruptly. Most prerecorded music naturally fades in and out, so the recording engineer should not fade it further unless they wish to start it in the middle or end it prematurely.

feed-back - An annoying high-pitch whistle that is created when a microphone picks up the sound coming through a speaker and sends it back through the amplifier system over and over. The effect snowballs until the limits of the system are reached (at which point a speaker or power transistor may blow).

line in (aka. "auxiliary in") - A connector (or pair of connectors) on the back of a device (tape deck, equalizer, etc.) to which a cable can be attached that will tie together another piece of equipment. For example, to copy a tape, you can hook up the line-out jacks of the tape deck that has the original tape to the line-in jacks of the tape deck that will be making the duplicate. *See also voltage levels.*

line level - A standard voltage level utilized to feed audio signals from one piece of equipment to another. See voltage levels.

line out - *See line in.*

microphone level - *See voltage levels.*

mixer - Term used refer to either a mixing console or microphone mixer depending on the context.

mixing - A recording technique whereby two or more channels of audio signal are combined into one.

mixing console (or mixing board) - A piece of equipment used to control a number of sound levels at the same time. A typical console will accept six or eight different inputs and combine them according to the operator's controls, sending the mixed levels to one or more outputs. Usually, each of the input channels will be capable of handling either *microphone level* inputs or *line level* as desired; however, it may be set up so that only certain channels will take certain types of inputs. There are also special mixing consoles made for the purpose of accepting inputs directly from stereo turntables. Trying to use turntable inputs for anything else will not produce desirable results.

monitor speakers - A set of speakers placed on stage for the benefit of the actors. This is often necessary in larger halls where the main speakers are sometimes isolated from the stage (by distance, curtains, etc.). Hint: If there is a danger of the monitor speakers causing feed-back, then try adjusting the tone controls on the amplifiers that drive the monitors so that the bass is not as loud as the treble. (See 7.2, Speaker Placement)

mono / monophonic. - A single source of sound, as opposed to stereophonic or quadraphonic which deliver 2 or 4 *channels*, respectively.

multi-track recording - A recording technique where different channels of audio which will eventually be mixed together are first recorded onto different tracks of an intermediate tape.

patch cord - A short cable used to connect together two pieces of equipment (or in rare cases to connect a piece of equipment to itself). Most stereo systems use patch cords (with RCA type connectors on each end) to connect the tape deck to the receiver.

pre-amp - An amplifier used to boost a signal from microphone level, such as from a microphone or turntable, to line level. *See voltage levels.*

receiver - A stereo system component that contains both a radio tuner and a power amplifier (among other features). It may or may not also contain a pre-amp specifically designed for a turntable input.

recording techniques - The three basic techniques used for preparing most masquerade show tapes are mixing, splicing, and multi-track recording. (See chapter 4)

requirements analysis - The first phase of a four-phase method for designing and implementing projects. The idea was originally developed for the field of software engineering (computer programming) but is applicable to virtually any project. The other three phases are preliminary design, detailed design, and coding (implementation). The work involved with each phase includes such aspects as systematically conforming to each previous phase and determining how the next phase it to be tested.

splicing - A *recording technique* that is the action of piecing together different sounds, one right after another, into one cohesive program. It can be accomplished either physically with a razor blade and splicing tape or by pausing the recorder while the next piece is cued up.

stage directions - (right, left, up, down) "stage left" and "stage right" are from the actor's point of view as they look upon the audience. "House left" and "house right" are from the audience's point of view; therefore, house left equals stage right and vice versa. "Up stage" is towards the back wall; "down stage" is towards the audience. (Up & down originate from the days when audience seating was level while the stage angled up.) To "up stage" an actor is to do silly things behind their back as they face the audience (which puts you up stage of them).

track - Most tape recorders are capable of recording two or more channels worth of audio information on the same piece of magnetic tape. They do so by dividing up the tape into tracks. For example, with a stereo tape deck, signals from the left channel might be recorded onto the lower half of the tape while right-channel signals are recorded on the upper half. One recording technique called multi-track recording, takes advantage of being able to record different items on the different tracks and then mixing them together at a later time. *See also dubbing.*

voltage levels. - Different types of audio equipment work at different voltage levels. This means that, for example, you cannot hook a microphone directly into a power amplifier without first going through a pre-amp. Microphones, turntable needles, and guitar pick-ups all operate at microphone level (measured in millivolts) and require some sort of pre-amp to bring them up to line level (around 10 volts). Line level signals can be passed through equalizers and reverb tanks, fed into tape recorders and powers amps, etc. Power amplifiers, in turn, boost the signals to where they can drive speakers. Usually, only line level signals can be mixed together with a simple *Y-adapter*, while microphone level signals need to be mixed with a microphone mixer made for the purpose (unless they are first amplified to line level).

Some pieces of equipment have pre-amps and/or power amps built into them. Portable tape recorders and most tape decks, for example, have pre-amps in them to allow for a microphone or two to be directly attached. If your tape recorder has a built-in speaker, then it must also have a built-in power amplifier to drive it (albeit a small one).

X Adapter - A special patch cord than can be created by connecting the bases of two Y-Adapters This is useful for combining both *channels* of a stereo recording into a mono signal, and sending the mono signal to both output channels. Warning: some equipment (notably turntables) will not work properly if connected with a Y-adapter.

Y Adapter - A special patch cord than can be used to connect two inputs to one output or vice versa. This is useful for combining both *channels* of a stereo recording into a mono signal. Warning: some equipment (notably turntables) will not work properly if connected with a Y-adapter

MASQUERADE AUDIO HANDBOOK
- ORGANIZER'S SUPPLEMENT

By Craig L. Jones
Second Edition, 17 January 1988

Table of Contents

This is a supplement to the handbook intended for costumers who enter a masquerade event.

1 - Introduction

1.1 - How to Read this Supplement. This supplement assumes at least a familiarity with the main handbook. For example, there are references to terms and concepts in this supplement that are defined in the glossary that appears in an appendix at the end of the handbook. If a word or phrase appears in italics, then it is defined in that glossary. The first time you encounter such a word, you might need to look it up, but thereafter, you will know its meaning and not be subjected to it again and again.

1.2 - Intended Readership. This supplement is for anyone involved in running a masquerade event. Obviously, the sound technician will be the one to get the most out of this supplement; however, anyone who has to work with the audio tech may wish to skim this material so that they will at least know what is presented here. That way, for example, when the audio technician says that they need to set up the sound table in what appears to be the best seat in the house, you'll know they are not being vain, but rather that they must be able to hear what the audience hears or else what the audience hears won't be any good.

2 - The Basics of Playback Equipment for the Stage

I've learned the hard way that the best setup is a simple one. Things can get going fast and furious at times, and the more complicated you make things the greater the chance of mucking it up. This is especially true in a situation such as this, where not only are there no rehearsals, but you are lucky if you even get to listen to the soundtracks before you have to play them live.

2.1 - Amplifiers, Speakers, and Cables. For a small, regional convention, you can probably get away with using a good home stereo, but if you are in a larger hall, say, an audience size in excess of 200-250, then you will want to rent something more powerful. Be sure to bring a diagram of the hall with you to the rental company (complete with measurements and the intended locations of the stage, sound table, and podium) so that you can be sure they supply the right kinds and amount of cable, stands, etc.

Getting enough cable is, obviously, very important. If you are using an amplifier that is built in to the mixer (or if, for some other reason, you plan to have the amplifier back at the sound table), then you will need enough cable to go from each speaker all the way back to the amplifier. Exception: If you are running mono (as you should), then you MAY be able to get away with using less cable by connecting the two speakers together and then running only one cable back to the amplifier. However, you MUST make sure the equipment you get is designed to work that way. Check with your rental agency.

If your amplifier and mixer are separated (as with the amplifier being up under the stage and the mixer being back at the sound table), then you will need enough cable to connect the line-out of the mixer to the line-in on the amplifier. Microphone cable is usually used for this purpose, along with appropriate adapters (if necessary) at each end.

2.2 - Cassette Decks or CD Players. (*This is old-school advice, of course.*) No matter what grade of amplifier equipment you are using, a standard home CD player will work, or a standard home cassette deck will do nicely to play the tapes. Be sure to bring two such decks or players if possible, even if you only intend to use one, because if a CD does not play or a tape jams it will be quicker to switch to the other unit.

2.3 - Mixing Consoles. Whether or not you need a mixer depends on just what you are trying to accomplish. If all you are after is to be able to play any tapes or CDs that the contestants supply, and you are satisfied with using the house system for any microphones, then you will not need a mixer at all. You can simply connect your (one) cassette deck or CD player directly into the amplifier (via the line-in or auxiliary-in jacks) and use its volume control to set the sound level and control fading out after each entry. Note: in case you are worried, having only one cassette deck or CD player is perfectly adequate as there will be sufficient time between contestants to switch media (provided you have them all cued up and ready to play).

On the other hand, if you are like me and you bring a whole slew of music and sound effects tapes or CDs so that you can (1) play music during the preshow and intermission(s), (2) play music to introduce the judges, etc. (3) play fanfares and drum rolls, and (4) (optional) play raspberries, and explosions when the MC bombs-out with their puns, then you will want to have both of the two cassette decks or CD players you brought be live at the same time, and have the ability to cross-fade them. This requires a mixer.

You will also need a mixer if there are any microphones that need to be amplified through this system. You may be content to use the house system for the MC's microphone, but if there is no decent house system, or if you want to be able to control the MC's microphone from the sound table, then you will need a mixer to handle it.

Your main concern when renting a mixing console will probably be making sure they don't give you one that is too fancy. Mixers can be very complicated, with many, many knobs and switches that are labeled in anything but plain English. Once again, tell/show your representative exactly what you are trying to accomplish and make sure they show you exactly how to use each and every control. (Or, at least, that they set it up for you in advance and put pieces of tape next to each control to mark what the settings should be.) Note: There is a difference between a *mixing console* and a microphone mixer. A microphone mixer is usually too small for this kind of job as it will typically only have one *auxiliary input* if any, which is not capable of handling two cassette decks or CD players.

If you will be doing other masquerades in the future, you may opt to go out and purchase your own mixer. I use a six *channel* stereo mixer that I bought from Radio Shack when it was on sale for $60, and I find that it is more than adequate for any masquerade.

3 - Helpful Hints for the Audio Technician

3.1 - Sound Table Placement. My first choice for the location of the sound table is always out in the audience. There, I can hear what the audience hears and see what they see so I can adjust the quality of the sound accordingly. Of course, the layout of the hall will dictate whether or not I can be right in the middle and still let those behind me see, or if I have to be off to one side or all the way in the back. The only problem that I've found with this kind of location (besides the director yelling at me for taking up too much potential seating space) is that I am cut off from the backstage activity. Ideally, this calls for renting or buying a headset system so that I can be warned of last-minute changes, but having a personal gofer to run back and forth seems to work just as well, especially if I am as well prepared as I ought to be. Note: For those of you who are really serious, low power wireless headsets can be had for about $80 a pair.

3.2 - Speaker Placement. There are three considerations for the placement of speakers: making sure the people in the last row can hear without deafening the people in the first, making sure the high-pitch sounds aren't muffled, and making sure that the microphones don't pick up the sound and cause feed-back.

The first problem is easily solved by elevating the speakers above the heads of the audience; human bodies are not very good conductors of sound energy, and if the speakers are down at their level, then the sound will be absorbed before it gets to the back.

Elevating the speakers also happens to be a good solution for the second problem. Treble (high-pitch sound) emanates in a tight cone straight out in front of a speaker, while bass (low-pitch) emanates in a wide pattern (even wrapping around to the sides and behind). If the speakers were to be aimed into the audience instead of across the top of their heads, then the bass would get out, but the treble would be lost.

Avoiding feed-back is a matter of placing the speakers where microphones won't cross in front of them. Place the speakers in front of the stage (one on each side) rather than along the back wall.

If you are in a very large hall you may have problems with the contestants not being able to hear as well as the audience. If this is the case, you'll want to set up a couple of monitor speakers on stage. Again, be careful to aim them away from any microphones to avoid feed-back.

If your audience is situated with the stage at the end of the hall instead of on one side (that is, the audience is deep rather than wide), then you still have a problem of deafening those in the front while the back can't hear. So, you will probably want to add a second set of speakers. Place them one on either side of the audience about half-way down, and set their levels to be the same as the speakers up front. Make sure you use two amplifiers or an amplifier that is specifically designed to run two pairs of speakers. Don't just hook two sets of speakers together.

3.3 - Microphone Stand Placement. I always like to use microphone stands that have booms on them. This means that I can situate the stand on the floor in front of the stage and have the microphone reach over, thus avoiding the sounds of footsteps traveling through the stand itself to be picked up by the microphone. The same thing goes for the microphone on the podium in order to avoid picking up any noises that the MC might make.

3.4 – Stereo vs. Mono. I always use mono. Why? There are two reasons. The first is that stereo just doesn't work in a large hall. Only the people in the center of the audience will hear both channels evenly. Everyone else will mostly hear one channel or the other. The other reason is that sometimes contestants will turn in tapes that have music on one track and narration on the other. When I mix them together, sending both tracks to both speakers, the audience gets a better chance of hearing it all.

3.5 - Routing and Taping Down Cords. The main objective here is obviously to avoid having anyone trip over your cords. Duct tape is the best kind of tape for this purpose, but even it isn't perfect. No matter how well you tape down your cords, someone IS going to trip on them. Therefore, be sure include a loop of slack at either end of each span. That way, when it gets kicked up, the culprit/victim won't cause your whole sound system to come crashing down.

Use silver duct tape anywhere that people will be walking and reserve the use of black duct tape -- which can't be seen very well even when lit -- for when it is needed on the stage.

Another thing to watch out for when routing your cables is that microphone cables can, through inductance, pick up 60 hertz noise (hum) from power cables. I highly recommend that you route your microphone cables separately from your speaker and power cables and especially from any power cables feeding lights from a dimmer. Routing them on the other side of the aisle (i.e. a few feet away) will do nicely.

Backstage

-- Section 7 --

BACKSTAGE FOR LESS COMPLEX MASQUERADES

by Janet Wilson Anderson

The care and feeding of contestants from check-in through post -mortem.

What's It All About

A masquerade contestant when not competing, may be the sanest of individuals (except for their aberrant hobby). But under the stress of competition, even the calmest of us are apt to get nervous, panicky. even hysterical, and lose all sense and reason. That is why it is one of the major challenges of the Backstage Manager and crew to simplify the contestant's life as much as possible.

Your task is to provide information, help, and crisis control in a calm, soothing manner. A simple registration process, easy check-in, memory aids, backstage help of several kinds, a repair table, refreshments, ops/MC/ judges coordination, and gentle, but firm problem-solving, all contribute to ease the contestant's other worries and let them focus on the real source of stress - the presentation.

This is what the Backstage Manager and their staff do.

Staff Recruitment

1. If possible, the Backstage Manager should recruit the key backstage staff at least a couple of weeks in advance of the masquerade. Your key people are your Den Leader, repair table person check-in person and, for the larger masquerades (over 25 entries), your Sergeant-at-arms.

2. Send a confirming letter or message telling these folk what the layout of the facility is, where to meet on the night and what time to be there. You may suggest they wear dark, comfortable clothes - not costumes.

3. Put out the word to other people interested in helping with the masquerade to show up about 10 minutes before check-in is to start. These are your Den Helpers, and Pushers (the people who get the costumers physically on stage.

Setting Up the Backstage:

1. About 30 minutes to an hour before the contestants are due to arrive, set your den up backstage.

2. The Backstage Manager should give a thorough briefing to their crew before check-in starts. It should include stage layout, entrances and exits, catcher protocol, check-in procedure, repair table location, bathroom location, use of Den Helpers, care and feeding of costumers, photography situation, seating arrangements in the hall, where to go after the presentation, and use of badges as checker mechanisms. Walk them through the stage layout, traffic pattern to and from the stage and photo area so they know what to tell the contestants about their movements and seating, and location of other essential facilities (bathrooms, repair table, workmanship judging location).

3. Set up the backstage area:

A: Repair table - set out supplies

B: Food and water station - get out glasses, straws, food and drink

C: Set tables around the edge of the room for contestants to put their stuff on.

D: Set chairs in circles for contestants to sit on.

E: Put up large signs on the wall locating each contestant group by Den Leaders assignment. "**Entries 1 -5 here**," "**Entries 6-10 here**," etc. This helps contestants locate their Den Leaders, and helps locate the contestants when it's their turn to go on.

F: If there is to be workmanship judging, set up a small table in a well-lighted area out of the main traffic flow backstage for the workmanship judges. Label the location "**Workmanship Judging Here**."

G: Set up the check-in table just outside the green room main entrance. Put up a BIG "**Masquerade Check-In Here**" sign Have "staff" badges or labels or ribbons available to identify contestants' helpers accompanying contestants.

H. Put up "**No Smoking**" signs everywhere!

I. Put a sign up near the green room entrance saying "**RESTRICTED AREA - Contestants and Staff Only**." Assign a volunteer to stand door guard to keep out on-lookers. (Otherwise your green room will get overrun with photographers and other curious folk.) Everyone backstage should be identified - either as contestant or helper.

The Check-in Process

1. Make your check-in sheet just as soon as the running order of the masquerade is determined. List each entry by number, skill division, entry name and costumer name. Make several copies of this, since it is the running order of the masquerade and will be needed by check-in, Backstage Manager, Tech Head, audio, lights, and video staff and Sergeant-at-arms. Each judge should also get a copy, as should the judges' clerk.

2. Assign Den Leaders to contestants and list them on the check-in sheet. For an SF Masquerade, where last-minute repairs or assembly are the rule, you will want one Den Leader for each 5-6 entrants. For a historical masquerade, where the costumes generally arrive in a more complete state, one for every 8-9 should do.

3. Make a file card for each entry. Write the entry number on it (big) and the Den Leader's name (small).

4. Give your checker(s) the check-in list and the file cards. As a contestant arrives, they are checked off; they are told who their Den Leader is and where to find them, and they are told to **HANG ON TO THE CARD UNTIL JUST BEFORE THEY GO ON STAGE.** If they have brought their own helpers, label them before they get backstage.

5. The Backstage Manager should periodically check with the check-in desk to see who hasn't shown up yet. If someone hasn't arrived by five minutes to show time, the Backstage Manager should inform the Masquerade Director, so the MC, judges and tech crew can be informed.

Den Leaders

1. Give each Den Leaders a very conspicuous badge that says "DEN LEADER NOs. X to Y".

This will help the contestant find their Den Leader. The Den Leader should write the contestants' numbers on their badge and mark them off as they show up.

2. A Den Leaders is the main line of communication between the Backstage Manager, Masquerade Director and the contestants. If something comes up that all should know, the Masquerade Director. will tell the Backstage Manager. who tells each Den Leader who tells their group. They should let the group know all relevant information about traffic flow, location of essential facilities, seating, and stage layout. They should be sure contestants know the sequence of events. Even if they should already know this, the Den Leader should tell them again!

3. A Den Leaders' primary responsibility is to serve their group of contestants. They should know the location of the repair table. They should offer them liquid refreshment or munchies. Some costumers have been known to forget to eat or drink for hours before and during a Masquerade, leading to a seriously-depleted state. Others can't face the thought of eating or drinking, so a Den Leader should always ask. If they think someone is about to pass out, they should call for the Backstage Manager immediately.

4. If a costumer needs considerable help in getting ready (more than a couple of minutes) a Den Leader should call for a Den Helper to devote themself to that costumer's needs. This ensures that the rest of the group do not get neglected while they help just one person for a long time.

5. If there is official photography before the masquerade, it is the Den Leader's responsibility to shepherd their den through photography. They may use the floating Den Helpers to assist them in this. They can mark through each contestant's number on their badge when they have been photographed to keep track. If photography is afterwards, they should accompany their group there and help them through the line.

6. A Den Leader should be alert to problems and notify the Backstage Manager as soon as they spot one. If one of their contestants is going to have a special entry or exit need that they haven't already identified, they should let the Backstage Manager know so the helpers and catchers are alerted.

7. They should always <u>identify the problem costume by entry number</u> (check the contestant's card for this), since this number is the key one for all concerned.

8. A Den Leader should know all of the group by name and number. When it is time to assemble to go on stage, it is the Leader's responsibility to deliver everyone to the Sergeant-at-arms for line-up. If someone is missing, they go and track them down.

9. A Den Leader should watch over the group's belongings, especially those items like glasses or watches shed at the last minute before going on stage. Remember to give them back, too.

10. A Den Leader accompanies the den to the stage for the competition, and after the last one is on stage, meets them either at photo or at contestant seating. They should stay with the den during the judging intermission and help them back on stage if they win.

11. If there is stage access for practice before the competition, a Den Leader should let the den know about it. They may help them themselves, or draft a Den Helper to do so.

Den Helpers

Den Helpers perform two main functions:

1. Before the masquerade starts, they are the floating staff. They help with lengthy assemblies/repairs. They help people on and off stage during practice. They serve as gofer for the Backstage Manager. They run the errands to ops, security, venue staff. They fill in wherever an additional pair of hands or feet is needed. They too should have large conspicuous badges, so everyone knows who to grab to get some help. You need one for every two Den Leaders.

2. When the masquerade starts, three or four of the Den Helpers - the big strong ones - will assist people to get onto the stage with their costumes intact (not to mention their persons). These Helper's will lift trailing draperies from the front to help people upstairs and lift heavy props. These Helpers are called Pushers, and report to the Sergeant-at-arms.

Sergeant-At-Arms

The Sergeant-at-arms serves four main functions:

1. They keep order backstage and evict un-authorized visitors.

2. They are the one charged with getting the contestants lined up in order to go on.

A few minutes before starting time, they should ask the Den Leaders of the first group to bring their den to the staging area. Using the numbered cards, they line the den up in order. They are responsible for keeping the line moving and being sure that each den is called in time. If there is a problem and the sequence has to be changed, they notify the Backstage Manager, who in turn gets word to the MC and tech crew. The MC will, of course, announce the change to the judges and the audience to avoid confusion.

3. In large masquerades, they are on head-set with the tech crew, keeping them informed of who is up next and when they should start the tech for that entry.

4. They are is in charge of the pusher crew who actually move contestants on to the stage.

During the Masquerade

The Backstage Manager is the liaison with the tech crew. They are the person who lets the crew know when each costumer is ready to go on and the one who calls a halt if trouble arises. They are the last person the contestant sees before going on stage. They will have the check-in list back from the checkers, and as each contestant hands them their numbered card, they check to be certain it is the right person. And they get to wish each contestant their final "Good Luck!"

Judges' Clerk

This helper is assigned to make the judges' lives easier. Their functions:

1. Before the judges are due to arrive, they set up the judges' table with water, glasses, pens, small flashlights, and a copy of the running order list for each judge.

2. They deliver the judges' forms to them at the start of the masquerade, in the proper order. If the sequence changes before the start of masquerade, they will fix the paperwork.

2. While the judging is going on, the judges' clerk tallies up each contestant's score and separate the forms into piles by Division. It helps to have a calculator!

3. At the end of the masquerade, the judges' clerk sorts each division pile into order with the highest scores on the top of the stack. They accompany the judges to their deliberations, but, of course, say nothing.

4. They take note of each award as it is decided. They makes sure the proper award title is listed on the correct form and in the correct order for delivery to the MC. At the end of the judging, they collect all the forms, deliver the award forms to the MC, and return all others to either the Backstage Manager or the Masquerade Director for destruction. They also retrieve any reference attachments and bring them backstage to be collected after the award ceremony.

5. They provide the Masquerade Director with a complete list of all award winners, with full names and entry names.

After the Masquerade

1. Den Leaders check to make sure each of their groups has gone through the photo line, if there is one. They can help hold paraphernalia, arrange draperies and help the contestant move through each posing station. The Den Leaders also return any materials left with them.

2. When the judges return to announce the awards, Den Leaders should make sure all of their contestants reassemble where they can hear the awards. Cheering loudly when one of your group wins is perfectly acceptable Den Leader behavior.

3. After all is over, the Backstage Manager and crew clean up the green room. Repair table supplies are inventoried so items used up can be replaced for the next show. Signs are taken down and any left-behind articles retrieved. The Backstage Manager should turn these over to the Masquerade Director who can take them to the costumers' post masquerade party, if any, to the masquerade post-mortem, or to the convention's lost and found.

Backstage Manager – Other Duties

1. Backstage Manager's main function is to deal with problems as they arise - **CALMLY**. It is they who sets the tone for the crew and the entire backstage area. If you panic, don't let it show!

2. It is also critical that the Backstage Manager be highly visible and most importantly, **available**. You can't solve a problem if you can't be found. With a good crew, these will be minimal, but there will always be some last-minute crisis for you to deal with.

3. The Backstage Manager should be notified of any persons not wearing a badge or competing. They will query the interloper and determine their status. Crew members should always refer interlopers to the Sergeant-at-arms or Backstage Manager who can even summon Security if necessary.

4. After the Masquerade, the Backstage Manager will warmly and personally thank every member of the crew for their help!

5. The Backstage Manager should show up at the masquerade post-mortem, if any, and invite suggestions from the participants on what went right and what can be improved. **Again, gracious thank-you's will help ensure the return of good crew for the next show!**

Last Words

No one can ever predict all the things that can happen at a Masquerade. As one Masquerade Director put it: "It's a big show where there's no rehearsal; the cast and crew meet each other for the first time that night, and you have no idea who's is going to do what. It's a wonder things go as well as they usually do!" The key thoughts are:

PLAN

ANTICIPATE

COMMUNICATE

and most importantly,

RELAX!

Happy Masquerading!

BACKSTAGE JOB DESCRIPTIONS

by Cat Devereaux

This document covers people's jobs and the items that are required for a large (regional) masquerade or a Costume-Con, from Backstage Manager all the way down to the gofer crew. Most of the jobs are written up as handout sheets for the persons who will perform the jobs. The sheets list not only their duties but the items that they will need to secure to complete their jobs.

This document does not cover front-of house except to discuss how the functions interrelate with back stage.

A lot of this is borrowed and expanded from Janet's Backstage at the Masquerade (which is for smaller cons) and from learned experience (under Janet's tutelage). The items required vary little except in quantities (crew and supplies). I am a firm believer in dividing tasks and then leaving the person to do the job with minimal interference (no matter how much my hands may itch to get in there and 'help'). The job divisions are my backstage preference and are based partially on my theatre experience. (The methods seem to work, and my crew normally has very high morale.)

For any size con, it should be the goal of the Backstage Manager to remove all the mundane setup worries and let the Masquerade Director concentrate on registration and, later, running the masquerade.

At the end of the description of the backstage are some rules for backstage behavior and the Masquerade Director that I hope will be taken in the helpful spirit they are presented!

Backstage Manager – Job Description and Duties

You are either a masochist with a power complex, or a poor person who owes the Masquerade Director a blood debt. Or maybe you were foolish enough to volunteer for this spot? Regardless of what you are telling yourself, you are not stupid. The Masquerade Director picked you because they need someone to handle all the silly backstage details that can hang up a masquerade.

You are in charge of selecting backstage crew and coordinating all events backstage. Use this document and the attached handouts only as a guide. No two people will do backstage the same.

From the day you are asked to assist with the masquerade, determine exactly how much of the duties will be yours. Show-time is the wrong time for major (or even little) surprises.

The duties listed here assume that you will be removing as much as possible from the Masquerade Director's shoulders. If the Masquerade Director is expecting too much, say so. There is no hard and fast way to break out the tasks. However, the more you oversee the less you have to worry about if the Masquerade Director must handle major emergencies from the con committee, venue, and contestants.

Before the Convention

Check out the venue yourself and anticipate everything that could go wrong. Figure out traffic patterns and check ceiling and door heights. Don't forget to check the chandelier height for both the stage and hallways. Problem? Bring it to the Masquerade Director's attention.

Is the venue union? What are your limitations if you must get something done?

Where is the green room? What hours will you have it? For a large con with the masquerade starting at 8 P.M., standard call time (6 P.M.) should not be an acceptable answer. Main contestant call may be two hours before the masquerade. A lot of people need an area to set up in earlier. Main crew should be there 20-30 minutes early. For a Costume-Con try to get the green room for the whole con. If not, consider the amount of time required for cleanup (after the fashion show) and pre-judging (for the Historical if it will be done in the green room). Also. the Fashion Shows need much more time for make-up.

Figure out your backstage layout. Get your request in early for the number of tables you will need. (Check-in, repair, make-up.) Don't forget to check out power outlets. Fashion Shows need trash cans and extra lighting. You will want some kind of a mike backstage. Clothes racks? Full length mirrors? Iron and ironing board? Privacy screen?

Start begging tech crew for a backstage monitor so that people can watch the masquerade and a headset for yourself. Be happy if you can get the monitor for your people. You will seldom end up with a headset. (Depending on resources and how far away the green room is, you may get one.)

Start thinking of worst-case scenarios and plan strategies to handle these. What if you lose your green room? What if you lose some of your pipe and drape? What if it rains? What if the con is twice the size originally planned? (Use your imagination and your nightmares. These have all happened.)

Do not let yourself get volunteered for any other duties during the con beyond assisting the Masquerade Director at registration. Because of the emergencies that come up, you will not have time.

Go over the backstage snack menu with the Masquerade Director.

You will probably be the one getting the items. Foods need to be a combination of sugars, salts, bulk and no-lead versions of the same items. Gatorade is a must for long masquerades. They should all be bite size, non-sticky, non-messy, non-crumbly. The same rules/reasons that apply to gooey costumes apply doubly to snacks. (Don't be nice and bring dip. It will only end up dripping down someone's costume.) Gets lots of bendable straws.

Work as an assistant for anything the Masquerade Director wishes ahead of time. If possible, practice with your Masquerade Director at smaller cons. Dress rehearsals always help iron out the kinks.

If you are not going to interact with your Masquerade Director(s) much before the con, send them a memo telling them what you are planning to provide and asking for input. If you do not hear from them, do not assume everything is all right. Find out how much experience they have had as Directors and anything special they are requiring from you. Avoid surprises. Communicate!

Volunteers for crew have a tendency to keep changing. Planned costumes can crash and burn (and then you have great helpers), or may rise like a Phoenix from the ashes (then you don't have them), or mundane considerations such as jobs or finances or health may interfere. Stay prepared to improvise. You never know what lurks in the woodwork.

During the Convention

Separate out all your stationary supplies as soon as possible. Whatever you estimate you need in pens, get twice that amount. Everyone 'borrows' from backstage, and judges 'eat' pens. These should all be stored in a special large bag that your crew heads are familiar with. Do not use an open container such as a cardboard box. You cannot afford to have your supplies grow legs and run away.

By now the convention schedule should have solidified enough that you can finalize call times for your crew if you have not done so yet. When setting up times, consider how they are going to get meals. They are normally working by the time the con suite opens to feed the regular volunteers. What are the snack bar's hours?

Start checking-in your volunteers as they get there. (Until you do this, you do not have any idea what kind of havoc weather and personal items might wreak on your crew assignments.) Confirm that they can still work the position agreed upon. If some of your main people sometimes arrive late, call them the week before the con and confirm they will be working their spot. Scrounge all the extra help you can from those near registration. It's a great way for 'newbies' to get involved and to see the costumes up close.

A good way to track crew for a Costume-Con is to list all names of volunteers and draw columns for each event. Write down positions or check off the square for helpers. Use dashes to denote a person is definitely not available for an event. Use stars to denote people you know are good. Wave your list under the noses of other experienced con people and star anyone they tell you is experienced. Check off people as you see them at the con. These lists will be a life saver as the con progresses and brain fading fatigue sets in.

When members of your crew are helping you before the con, be kind -- pace them. Throw them out for food, rest and to see parts of the con (especially the out-of-towners). Get more people to do short shifts with you. Don't burn anyone out the day before, if you can avoid it.

Post call times and places as soon as possible. Crew call times should be before contestant call except for the helpers. Be sure to include times for stage setup if it will occur at a time other than just before the masquerade. Notify people ahead of time when you plan to strike the stage area. Five people will get to the parties only a half hour late; three will never see the parties. If there are multiple shows, house crew needs to be there only an hour before if there is no change in the stage setup for the later masquerades.

Get to know the actual part of the venue that does water setup. Five dollar tips do wonders. You will never be out of water. It is safer for them to keep the tables clean and water plentiful. Your own people will have a tendency to rush and will not be carrying the water on sturdy carts. Find out where you can get water if the venue is slow. Pass this along to your assistant (then between the two of you, there may be water all the time.)

Do your planned traffic patterns exist? If you will be using kitchen access ways, get to know the people back there. Mark the path to the masquerade stage with many large arrows. (Use duct tape and/or the neon security tape.) Are the floors dry? Are the aisles clear? (Keep checking these up to the start of the masquerade as it can change without notice.)

Monitor the amount of people signing up for the masquerade. How are guesses and crew estimates holding up? If you are going to run short of crew, now is the time to start groveling near registration. Abandon your pride. Get crew any way you can. The more people the work load is spread across the better the experience is for everyone.

When registration closes, assist the Masquerade Director with the line up or stay out of the Director's way. It is their choice. Now is no time to jiggle their elbow. Be around to provide emotional support if required because this is normally the point when the Director's panic attack sets in. You must be calm now. (You had your panic attack before you started groveling for crew. You are not allowed a second.)

If you are within an hour and a half of contestant call and do not have a running order, hunt down the Masquerade Director! Help them in any way you can to finalize the list. The moment it is done, get a copy to tech! They need it first. (If you cannot find the Masquerade Director, do not panic. Get ruthless. No list is normally the sign of much worse problems. Does the masquerade need to be postponed an hour? Find the Con Chair. Make the decision before the con people break for dinner and announce it in every room and hallway.)

The running list should have costume name, contestant's name, number in group and experience level. If it doesn't, fill in the information. Split the dens at this point into as many dens as you have Den Leaders and Helpers to handle. Keep in mind contestants who may have problems with one another and divide the dens at that point. Dens of five to seven contestant numbers are the average. However, if there are a large number of people in a contestant group, move the diving point around so that people numbers are balanced fairly evenly. Do not just arbitrarily assign Den Leaders to groups.

If all your den people are experienced, throw all caution and pre-planning to the wind. Let them pick their dens on a first-come-first-pick basis. Let them know ahead of time and some will be there a half hour early. (They can help with set-up.) Others do not really care. This method normally means... last one there gets the children's group.

If you are not familiar with your den people or know you are going to have hot spots, use more scientific reasoning. Give new Den Leaders a smaller den with mostly journeymen or experienced novices (include a knowledgeable Den Helper). Try not to give the novice den person any master-level entrees. Masters have more detailed and complicated requirements and expect a number of things automatically from Den Leaders. Masters normally are more uptight because they have much more 'invested' in the masquerade and may require the gentle sledge hammer approach from someone they are familiar with. Ask for a volunteer for the kids' den.

Give the last den (normally including the grand opera set) to a very experienced Den Leader. These people often have the most chaos going on around them and it takes an experienced band to maintain order. If you have any personality conflicts within a den, warn the den person ahead of time quietly. (The Masquerade Director should have already warned you.)

When doing a Fashion Show, dens should be larger since almost all the costumes are individuals. Divide the groups at pod breaks (sections in the scrips such as casual wear, evening gowns). Have check-in assign each den a specific helper to be the assistant den person. Fashion Shows require splitting dens in half early on to handle double side entrances. Instruct the Den Leader to take one half and the Helper the other, or else the far side group will be neglected.

Just Before Contestant Call:
Recheck the green room and your stage. Has anything changed? Is tech going to be ready on time? How late? Do you really have kitchen access? Is the way clear?

Have your early arrival helpers set up munchies. Don't you do it! Now is the time to regain your composure and modify your personality from accommodating gofer to that of a benevolent dictator. You have a backstage to run.

Your den and check-in people should arrive early. Give them a quick briefing on backstage rules and any problems you are expecting. Tell them where the restrooms are that the contestants will be using. Warn them that, if they are aware someone's costume or presentation will break some of the show rules, they should discreetly notify you so that you may handle the smaller problems and pass the bigger ones to the Masquerade Director.

Now is the time for the den people to stake out their den areas. (The index cards with their den numbers should be waiting for them at check-in.) If there is enough time and space, set the chairs in den circles. It has a tendency to keep the group together better than stringing a den out across one wall. (Dens that chat together have a tendency to stay in one location.) Have an extra running order that can be cut apart by check-in so that each den can have their piece to track their group.

If you are behind on setup, have check-in stop all traffic at the door. Take the extra five minutes and get organized. (You may never catch up if you do not.)

(Side note: This is the point where you take off the kid gloves when dealing with the crew. You will have to work with just the number that has shown up. They volunteered to help, so do not feel guilty if you must now run them into the ground. Make your request with an honest thank-you, then push them!)

Contestant Check-in Call

Your main job is to be available and fight any small fires that arise (which means you will be very busy). Keep a couple of runners near you. If you hang out near check-in, the fires have a tendency to come to you.

Use check-in as your base of operations for information. They should have the master copy of the backstage list because they are stationary and you are not.

When the stage is ready, take all your den people and give, them a walk through. Update them on all general announcements. If the contestants do not hear you, they will be able to get the information from their Den Leader.

Make announcements when and as required. Workmanship judging: where, what? Judging photography: where? Official photography: where, when?. General photography: where, when? Contestant seating: is there any, where? Awards: where, when pick-up? Traffic patterns. Stage: markings, odd areas, final run-through times. Timing: adjusted start time, five minute warning.

Confirm that everyone has their job under control. HOWEVER, resist the urge to meddle. Let each person do their assigned job. They will learn from smaller mistakes and will get faster with practice. (Use your experience to recognize when they do need real help.)

If an errand is too important for a runner to handle, formally notify check-in and your assistant that you are leaving. Your assistant is in charge until you get back.

Follow up with check-in as to how many people have shown. If it is a half hour until show time, check with the Masquerade Director about the no-shows. Why are they late? Let your den people know you know.

As you are reviewing people who have arrived, handle weapons check. You (or your appointed Weapons Master) must check out all contestants who are wearing ANY kind of weapon. Any not being used in the presentation must be peace-bonded (string tied around the blade and sheath. Those being used must be checked to confirm they are constructed sturdy enough for what is planned. Take the contestants to a safe area of the backstage. Have them go through their presentation slowly then at standard speed. If the spacing is marginal, get time on the stage to have them run through it there. If an item or act will not meet safety standards and cannot be fixed/changed, you have the authority to pull that piece/part. If you have problems, have a runner get the Masquerade Director. Safety is always your number one concern!

A half hour before show time, remind your den people to link their dens with the one in front of them. Large costume or setup problems? Can your repair crew still pull off a miracle? Give that group all the resources you can spare. However, do not neglect the rest. Does the group need to pull out?

Any last-minute pull-outs? Your tech liaison can coordinate this with the various tech people. Send a two or three tag helper to notify the Masquerade Director and the MC.

If by some unlikely chance all contestants are there and ready ahead of time, notify the Masquerade Director (who may drop dead of shock!). Send a runner to the Director when everyone is ready whether you are on time or late.

The Masquerade Director may give you a start deadline. Obey!

Quickly check your dens. Will anyone not be able to meet the deadline? Push the marginal ones! They must start making decision to go with part of the costume or to pull out. (Yes, you are being nasty here. Save your apologies for after the show. The director has dictated, you MUST comply.)

During the Masquerade

Give contestants a five-minute warning. Notify den people when to line up the dens.

If you are going to start the show without everyone ready and you feel there is a good chance a costume may crash and burn at the last moment, let everyone know. Give their den person an index card with a clearly printed message that states that #n is being pulled. If the contestant must drop out, the card is ready for the Masquerade Director to slip to the MC. If the person can be inserted into the show later, the choice and location is the Masquerade Director's call. Just provide another index card. Don't forget to have someone with a headset notify tech!!!!

What you will be doing during the masquerade is different every single time. If the Masquerade Director is not checking to see that everyone is in the correct order, you or your assistant should handle it throughout the show. If everyone is doing their job and there are only small problems, you may be able to take a breather. Boredom is the sign of a good crew. (Now is the time to review your crew for the next event while the crew's performances are still sharp in your mind.)

Start cleaning up if you have time.

If there is contestant seating in the audience, you and your assistant need to divide your concentration between the two groups. Your den people should be hanging around to be caring for the people but if they are not, draft people.

After the Masquerade

Thank your crew personally (then go back and thank them again). You want them to know that you really appreciate the fact that they ran themselves into the ground to assist with the masquerade. (You WILL need them for the next one.)

Snag those you need to help with cleanup. Do not try to do it all yourself! If the stage is being tom down that night, have them help with that too.

Next Day

Gather all your check-in forms together. Make a single page list of the times all your people worked. Don't forget pre-masquerade setup times during the day. Get a copy of the list to the con volunteer coordinator and the Masquerade Director so that all your people get credit for their work. Make sure you keep a copy for yourself. (Do this even if volunteers are supposed to be keeping track of their own time. If the con committee is sticky about signatures, have the Masquerade Director sign it.) Make any notes about people you would like to move up to positions of greater responsibility next time. (Do them now before the names blur together.)

Thank your crew again as you see them in the halls. Go to the post-mortem and learn for the next time.

If you could not prevent every disaster and force everything to run smoothly in spite of the fact that your crew consisted of volunteers assembled in only a few hours to put on such a major production, do not feel that you did your job poorly. There will always be things that could have been done differently.

Try the following criteria for judging how the masquerade went.

- Was the masquerade run at a level where contestant safety was the primary concern? (During masquerades that are a major disaster with the stage setup or backstage, this may be the only requirement. No part of a masquerade should go on if safety is ever uncertain.)
- Did the audience enjoy the show? (That's the point of the masquerade. Sometimes that is all you can hope for.)
- Did the contestants enjoy the show? (The masquerade went well.) There are almost always contestant problems that your crew must work on until the last moment. However, if the contestants can go on the stage in reasonably good moods, their presentations will pick up their extra energy.
- Did the crew enjoy the show? (The masquerade went great!) When making this decision, do not evaluate the mood of the crew heads... look to the helpers. The smiles on the exhausted faces can make the hassles of running backstage worth doing again!

Backstage Crew Job Descriptions - Introduction

This is a quick summary of crew requirements and how the people can be assigned. The numbers in (parens) are the number of badge ribbons (levels of authority).

Assistant Manager - (3) - For a large or complicated masquerade, the Backstage Manager will need an assistant. This person should know everything the Manager knows about the event, and be experienced enough handle problems. They may be lucky enough to spend the masquerade doing minor gofering for the Manager, or if things are falling to pieces rapidly, they may work extensively.

It is best if, as Backstage Manager, you have worked with the person in the past and they can read your mind so that they can be wherever you are not. However, this is not a requirement. They just need to be a good dependable gofer who can solve problems.

If you are doing multiple events (such as backstage managing an entire Costume-Con), give this person as much responsibility as they can handle. You will burn up before the weekend is out if you do not pace yourself and delegate responsibilities. In a major disaster scenario, this person may have to sub for you by the end of the con if you or the Masquerade Director must be elsewhere.

Den Leaders - (3) - Den Leaders are there to make the costumers' lives easier. They are supposed to be the sane support staff that keeps things calm, so the costumers can concentrate on their presentations. They are a channel of communication between the crew and the contestant, conveying necessary information to the entrant and relaying problems or questions upward. They are the watchdogs of the contestant's well-being, making sure that the contestant has liquids, is as comfortable as the costume permits, is assembled into the costume without bodily harm or damage, and is ready to go on stage in good order. They have charge of a group of entries, called a den, and are responsible for delivering each member of their den onto the stage in a timely fashion. After each entry in the den has presented, they are responsible for keeping track of them and rendering them any aid needed. They are the key to a smooth-running backstage and happy contestants.

Work on training den people on local cons. If you cannot get experienced people by con time, use theatre people even if they have never seen a convention before. (Just brief them well, especially on communication channels. They understand baby-sitting nervous cast members.) Find out ahead of time if you have den people who do not want to work with kids and those who do not mind handling the young ones!

Get a guesstimate of the number of entrants from the Masquerade Director. This will help you guess at the number of den people you will need. Plan five to seven groups in a den. Numbers will vary until you have a running list in your hands and can determine how many singles or "grand opera" groups you have. Work with the Masquerade Director to determine problem spots.

Den Helpers - (1 or 2 or 3) This is where all extra help goes. Experienced help should have two tags, as should con kids who are dependable. Backstage helpers come in two types: those assigned a specific Den Leader, and general runners. Big dens definitely need a helper full time. If possible, give every den at least one attached helper. However, there are seldom enough people for this. If a contestant group brings their own roadies, see if the roadies will help with the whole group. By masquerade time, miscellaneous check-in and Judging Photo team members can be reassigned to help those who have limited sight lines and need someone with them for the trek to the ballroom. The general helpers are often those with more experience, able to do whatever is required.

Check-in Head - (3) - Main check-in will be in charge of tracking contestants, backstage crew and (unless other arrangements have been made) photo people.

This person is also in charge of supervising your security at the green room door. This person needs to be authoritative to keep people out. This person does not have to have heavy con experience if they have been well briefed and cannot be bullied. This spot can also be filled by an experienced con person who may not be able to be physically active. Since this job ends at the time the masquerade starts, this person can watch the masquerade up front if they wish. (Work this out ahead of time with them.)

Check-in Head will also have all extra stationery supplies and miscellaneous equipment. They must be able to be at the green room at least 15 minutes before the actual call time to get things sorted out for the helpers. If check-in is not ready, there will be a logjam at the door.

Check-in Assistants (2) - (1 or 2) One should help with the paperwork at the check-in desk as the check-in head's assistant. This spot doesn't need a lot of experience, so it can be a good spot to use an eager teenager. The second assistant will be physically blocking the door (since fire arrangements and wide costumes prevent blocking the door with the table) and helping keep out non-masquerade personnel. This person may be issuing the security badges for contestant's roadies as they enter. For Costume-Cons, this can be a general helper. For standard cons, use a security person (preferably one who can stay in the green room for the entire masquerade) to handle the door.

NOTE: If you are very short on crew, check-in is the first place to start reassigning people. However, you will lose a lot of security and you will not get the names or times worked of all your volunteers.

Judging Photo Team - (1 or 2) - Appoint a Head and Assistant Runner. The head person is in charge of the camera. The runner numbers the photos after they are taken and puts them in order. If well briefed, these people do not need much experience. (Only one person is needed at smaller cons.)

Tech Liaison - (3) -This person is the runner between tech and backstage. Before the show, they communicate any changes to the tech head and deliver late media. During the show, they may be on headset to the tech head, telling them what entry is up next and when they are ready to start. It is preferable that tech picks this person, but it is not necessary. This person should be familiar with masquerade tech and may actually be part of the tech crew during the masquerade.

Repair Table Lead - (3) - This person supervises the repair table, and makes minor repairs for costumers. It is helpful if this person has a fair amount of costume construction experience, particularly with glues and tape.

Do NOT assume that this person is bringing a kit. Ask them! Also find out how much it will cost. (Their personal supplies must be replaced.) For big regional conventions, an assistant may be needed.

Make-up / Hair Supervisor - (3) - (Fashion Show only - general conventions should expect the costumers to take care of their own make-up/hair/wigs. The repair kit should include some minimal makeup supplies, such as spirit gum, but primarily for repairs - not full makeup jobs.) The head of this group needs as much experience as possible in fashion shows. They will normally coordinate their own people and supplies. However, clarify this point with them. (This falls back under the Fashion Show Coordinator area because they will be more acquainted with the models' needs.) Find out how many miscellaneous gofers they will need.

Duties of the Den Leader

Your job is to take care of the people in your den physically and emotionally. You are also the main line of communication between your group of contestants and the Masquerade Director, MC, tech and Backstage Manager. Your main link with the rest of the world will be the Backstage Manager. Make full use of runners.

You need to be available for the entire length of the masquerade through the judging. If you cannot be available the whole time, let the Backstage Manager know. It is better to assist in the training of a new Den Leader and leave the den in their hands than to pass off your den in the middle of the event. The contestants need the continuity.

Dress comfortably. You will be on your feet almost the entire time. You need full range of movement and should wear nothing that can interfere with the care of the costumes in your den.

Eat dinner before your call time. It will be your last chance until near midnight. You will need the energy. Forget your diet for the evening.

Make sure you arrive at check-in as early as possible. Your assistance is often needed in setting up the room. When you get your den badge, also pick up the index card that denotes your den. Divide up the room with the other Den Leaders. Post the den card up high in the middle of your area. Rearrange any chairs you need. Find out immediately where the repair table is and what kind of munchies and drinks are available for your people. Circle your chairs.

Check with Check-in. How many groups do you have? How many are in each group? What are their divisions? Novices are more likely to need your encouragement and support. They may want last minute hints on their presentation. Masters are more likely to arrive late and not stay in their dens. Check with the Backstage Manager; if she/he isn't worried about them, forget about them until a half hour before show time.

If anyone in your den has a tremendous amount to finish on their costume or takes a lot of work getting into it, get a Den Helper to work with them. You must be available to all your den. If you need more helpers than have been assigned to you, talk to the Backstage Manager about your situation. More help will be found for you or the problem will be handled.

If your den has children as entries separate from their parents, remind the parents that they are in charge of the child. Dens are not baby-sitting services. Taking care of a child during the hustle and bustle of masquerade is a full-time job and should be done by someone the child knows.

Get your people through judging photography as soon as possible. If the costumes are extremely bulky, notify the Judging Photo team and they will come to that costume.

If General Photo is open beforehand, get your early arrivals processed as soon as possible. If photo must be done at half-time, notify the Backstage Manager of anyone who should go through on the A-priority list -- those that are sweating their make-up off, heavily masked, cannot stand, etc.

Explain to your novices what workmanship judging is. Just parts of a costume can be submitted for judging, not the whole thing. Encourage anyone who has a special item to go up. This is a major point where you start giving your people emotional support. If someone does not want to go up, do not force the issue. They may have a very good reason for not wanting to get that close to a judge.

As soon as you have all your den together (and all the information), but not more than an hour before hand (contestants forget easily), brief your people about the stage layout, traffic patterns, any problems, contestant seating, how to pick up awards, etc. Before this point, you should have personally walked the area to the stage keeping in mind the items that will become obstacles to your group's costumes.

When the Backstage Manager announces the stage is set, take your den, in groups, to the stage. If all do not go, try to leave a Den Helper with them. Groups with complicated moves may want to do a quick run-through on stage. If contestants do not want to go to the stage, they may stay in the green room.

This is often a good time to find out about complicated entrances and exits. Let the Head Pushers know. Notify the pushers if their own ninjas will be getting them on and off stage. Also let the stage crew know if they are going to be leaving a lot on stage or putting some of their people in the front stage area. It helps the next setup to warn the crew in advance.

Watch your den to determine if anyone is in need of food or water. They get nervous and forget to eat or drink. Dehydration can be a major problem in any type of costume that covers most of their body. Especially watch novices. If their costume is hard to get out of, they may plan on not drinking until after the whole masquerade is over. Remind them they are sweating it out their pores. You do not want a contestant passing out on you before the end of the evening.

The other people that need watching for fluids are in master division and doing complicated costumes. They are normally doing this on little sleep, are incredibly nervous, and forget completely about themselves. Use your experience to determine how far you need to push the issue if they say they don't need anything. Get the Backstage Manager if needed.

Anyone in your group that has weapons with the costume must go through weapons check-out. This is sometimes the Backstage Manager or some another person. Check with the Backstage Manager. The contestants will often be required at that point to run though the presentation for weapons check-out.

Very occasionally, everything goes wrong as the show time approaches. The attitude of disaster often communicates down to the contestants. At times like this you may need to take a firmer hand to pull your group out of the chaos. Use your judgment and remember the show is for the audience as much as the people competing. Do what it takes to get them ready.

On rarer occasions, the Backstage Manager will tell you to herd them up, period. If someone is not going to be ready to go on stage, let the Backstage Manager know. The information will be passed on to the Masquerade Director who will make the decision whether the costume will be rescheduled or pulled. That judgment is final!

If you discover that any of your group is wearing a rented or bought costume, discretely notify the Backstage Manager. They will not be pulled from the line-up at this late time, but they will be disqualified. (This does not include their stage ninjas obviously not in full costumes.)

If anyone in your group is planning on violating any of the basic masquerade rules (funky substances, flame, etc.), work with them to make sure this does not happen. Example: they need to use a lighter in their routine -- teach them how to pantomime. Any problems, notify the Backstage Manager. **SAFETY for the people and for their costumes is your number one concern!**

About a half hour before the show, line up your people, then link your den with the one in front of you. This means, introduce the people to the person in front of them in their running order. A person in a mask, who can see very little, may still be able to follow the 'red and gold' in front of them if their helper disappears. Also, if the first person in your den knows what costume the last person is wearing in the previous den; they can line up behind that person when your den is called to get ready. You may be away on an emergency.

About fifteen minutes before starting, make sure that everyone who has left the den is back in it. Don't let anyone else take smoke breaks in distant hallways at this point. Try to wrangle your group back together. The Masquerade Director will make decisions concerning anyone who has not yet checked in. If you have lost people who checked in a long time ago, warn the Backstage Manager.

Once your people are lined up to go on, make sure they keep the volume level down. They are nervous and forget. Help calm them. Continue offering encouragement. If they need you to handle glasses and miscellaneous belongings, get them back to them as quickly as possible after they finish.

Once your den bas been on stage, do not completely abandon them. They may need watering. If all your group has been through all the general photo area, there will be little to do until the awards are given. At that point your main duties are normally traffic director and cheering your group on. After the awards sometimes people in your den need to be propped up with words of encouragement. If they are confused as to why they did not get an award, refer them to the judges.

If you are not totally burned out, stay and help wrap the backstage green room.

Duties of the Den Helper

Your job is one of a backstage gofer. You will be doing many tasks, but make sure that your previous tasks are done before being pulled away to another section. You should be dressed very comfortably, wearing no items that will get in the way of the costumes.

Be sure to pick up your badge at check-in.

Many of you will be assigned to a den to assist the Den Leader with the group. Do not allow yourself to be pulled out of the den without notifying your Den Leader. They are depending on you. In the den, you help in any way required to get the contestants ready. As the time for the masquerade nears, you may be specifically assigned to be the eyes and/or ears of a person in a large costume. Be sure to listen to the den briefings. You may need to repeat the instructions to a nervous contestant.

Some helpers are assigned as floaters. Be prepared to answer to any cry for "Den Helper" that you hear. Try to stay loose to act as runners. The Backstage Manager may assign you to someone or a special place as the time draws closer to the masquerade.

Some of the Den Helper floaters are specialized or experienced people. If you need help and cannot find someone to ask, locate a helper with a two or three ribbon badge. They can take care of the problem.

Your job is over when the people you were assisting no longer require your help. Many of the people with masks take them off during the judging. Get them water if they need it. Find out if they will need you once the awards start. If you must leave earlier, let your Den Leader know.

After the masquerade run-through, keep an eye out for Den Leaders needing help. They may need runners to communicate with backstage, they may need you to get the water pitchers refilled, etc.

If you see something that needs doing, and you're not in the middle of a project, use your initiative and do it. If you can't, pass the word.

Duties of Head Check-in

Supplies:

- Index cards, numbered for each entry (large print) and den # (small in corner)
- Index cards, with 'DEN' and the den number (large) and entry numbers (small in corer)
- Security badges for all workers, roadies; con security and photo people get a labeled security strip
- Extra index cards, magic markers pens
- Pad stapler
- Sticky notes
- Tape (whatever kind approved to be stuck on the venue walls)
- Worker check-in sheets
- Photo area check-in list
- Master check-in list (if just a copy of the running order, label it 'backstage master') list of groups that still need to sign release forms (& a copy of those forms) location signs (or index cards) for:
  - check-in here
  - workmanship judging
  - judging photo area
  - official photo area
  - no-smoking signs
  - (see the sign list for more signs)

Duties

It is your responsibility to check in contestants and workers. No one is allowed past you who is not authorized.

Be at the backstage green room at least 15 minutes before contestant call. (It never hurts to meet with the Backstage Manager earlier in the day and get some things taken care of earlier.) Do not allow any of the contestants in before the Backstage Manager tells you the room is open. Secure a table to work on and have it put by the door. Get set up. Put security tags on everyone who is already working in the room.

You should have at least one Check-in Assistant to stay with you. The ballroom will have their own check-in person who will get their materials, and be briefed, by you. If you are not ready to open when requested, say so.

When contestants enter, check them off the master list and give them their entry number card. Remind them to hang onto it until they go on stage. Tell them their den numbers and Den Leaders.

Point them towards their den. Make sure that they have all signed the entry form release, and judging photo money (if any) has been paid. (You will have lists.) Any roadies they brought with them must be tagged as ninjas.

Photographers using the photo area must also check in. Give them a photo tag. This allows them in the photo area only, not in the green room!!!!!!

The only people allowed in the room without security tags are the judges, MC, actual contestants, and working venue staff. Anyone else must be tagged. If you have any problems, notify Security or the Backstage Manager.

Also keep the entrance clear of people standing outside just yammering. Do not allow any smokers access to the room or allow them to stand right outside the door. It is too dangerous.

Even once everyone is checked in, stay on duty at least until the masquerade starts. Security will watch the room after that.

Remember to turn your supplies over to the Backstage Manager when it is all over.

You may be required to sign out when the masquerade is over and the workers have finished with clean-up. Check with the Backstage Manager before disappearing.

Duties of the Judging Photo Team

Supplies

- Polaroid camera, or digital camera and photo printer
- Film packs, or memory cards, printer paper and spare toner
- Pen that writes on Polaroids or prints
- Copy of the running order
- (Borrow the stapler from check-in)

Duties

Take a picture of each costumed group. In larger masquerades, the pictures help remind the judges exactly what the contestants were wearing. One person is the picture taker, the other is the runner and general gofer. Use either a Polaroid camera, or a digital camera and print the photos from the camera or memory card. If the camera cannot print directly, switch memory cards occasionally or alternate between two cameras so that printing and photography can take place at once,.

Arrive at the same time as the Den Leaders: Get your security tags and then find a wall. Because of space limitations, this is often the corridor between regular photo area and the green room. If you are not in the middle of a traffic pattern, you can use chairs to secure an area. Another good area is near where the Workmanship Judges are to be located. This way the costume only moves once. Your runner can also function as runner for the Workmanship Judges. Let them know you are available to help.

Check the number of contestants. Make sure you have enough film, or memory cards, paper, and toner for the contestants and a few mistakes. If not, notify the Backstage Manager immediately.

As soon as you are ready, let the Backstage Manager know the judging photo area is open.

Take one picture of each group. Many times, you will not be able to get all of the costume in. That is OK. If a picture is off center, that too is OK. These are just quick shots to help the judges' memories.

The assistant should label the picture with the number of the entry immediately. Check off that number on your copy of the running order. These should be stapled to the judging forms. The stapler should be at the check-in table. Or the photos may be put in a stack in numerical order.

When you get within about thirty minutes of the show, you should have all the pictures taken. If not, send your assistant around to the dens to check with the Den Leaders. You should stay at the photo area as late arrivals will be coming to you. In a few cases, you will have to come to the costumes, but do this after the main rush is over.

If for any reason you cannot get pictures of all the contestants, that is OK. Make sure that pictures you have taken are stapled to the judging forms and the forms end up on the judging table, or that the entire stack is given to the judges' clerk. This will require coordination with the judges' clerk.

A Few Rules for Backstage and Contestant Behavior

From the Backstage Manager to the Masquerade Director and contestants.

The following items may sound harsh and strict but all of these cause major logistic and/or crew problems. It will make sure that your contestants get out the door ready to go on stage regardless of what must be done to accomplish this. The contestants will be pampered and coddled as much as is humanly possible (because a happy contestant makes for a good show). However, I also stand behind my crew and support them if anything gets out of hand. Some of these may be solvable through various masquerade rules.

My crew and I will do the best job we possibly can but....

#1. We are not baby-sitters. Children are to be taken care of by their parents or their parents' arranged sitter, not one of the crew. If both parents and smalls are to be separate entries in the masquerade, keep this in mind. Work out an arrangement with the parents ahead of time. We will be pushed for time and may not be quite as polite as you wish. (A suggestion: put the smalls and parents is groups far apart number-wise. The Den Leaders can handle the disparity but the parents will have time to re-psych themselves up for their own performance after the little one's is over.)

#2. The crew are all volunteers and give of their time freely. They are not twelfth century serfs to be abused at whim. Yes, they will make some mistakes but they are doing the best they can with the time and resources they have. There has been an alarming tendency lately for some contestants to forget this. I understand that they are under a lot of pressure, but their demands will disrupt backstage. If there is an incident, I will politely remind the contestant causing the problem.

#3. Den Leaders and Den Helpers are there to help coordinate the entire group of contestants and help with last minute emergencies and small last-minute touches. This does not include major finishing work on a costume. There is not always time to pull a good helper out of the regular work group and assign them just to one person to spend an hour to finish dressing them. This has also been happening with more regularity at cons. When we try to explain we are short on time and help, these are often the ones that then fall into category #2.

#4, Photographers interfering with, or slowing down, preparations will be removed. This refers to the Photo Room people bleeding over into setup areas, and amateurs among those preparing to go on.

Before you throw this letter back at me and consider another Backstage Manager, remember what I said at the beginning: my crew and I will do all we can for the contestants but occasionally that may mean reminding someone of their manners. This will only be done for the overall good of the event.

We will work magic for you!

Masquerade Security Badges
TAG EVERYONE THAT WORKS FOR THE MASQUERADE!

Masquerade security and crew hierarchy usually has little to do with the standard con's setup, so badges can be a help to both security and masquerade personnel. When working with large groups of stage crew, it helps everyone to know the others' titles or experience levels.

A cheap and simple way is to use index cards with strips of neon plastic 1/2 inch tape attached to the bottom of the card to show a person's level. The cards, with the job title, can then be taped onto a person's con badge.

The Masquerade Director gets tagged with 5 strips of neon tape, department heads 4, den and crew leads 3. Helpers are normally 1 strip unless they are very experienced. Two strips is a good way to tag the younger crew that have a lot of experience and are dependable. Any experienced, dependable con person who does not have a specific title should get three strips. All helpers should understand that a 1 ribbon strip should follow the instructions of a 2 or 3, even if there is a 20 year difference in ages. (So hand out the extra strips sparingly.) However, tagging 'up' a deserving person can be a great morale booster.

Operations Manager will get 4 strips. Tech heads get 3. All other tech people should have at least two strips. Head Catcher and Front of House Manager get 3, catchers 2, ushers and walkers 1. Give the ballroom check-in clerk the badges for the front of house.

Roadies for a particular costume group should be given just a strip of plastic with 'ninja' written on it.

Authorized photographers and video people should be tagged with a 'photo' strip.

If you are running multiple events, (such as Costume-Cons) use a different color for each event. If a person is going to work an event the entire con, do all the ribbon colors together. They will wear the badge the entire con. (If nothing else, it makes a good souvenir or combat ribbon.)

Instruct security that during the masquerade and masquerade set-up, these tags override standard security marking for anything related to the masquerade. If the person requesting action is a 4-tag, the action should be followed as if the Masquerade Director was requesting it. Even tag Con Security with a strip to denote that they are working for the masquerade.

Do up most of the badges ahead of time or at least during the day. Do not leave them all for check-in to do at the last minute.

One more security item: If this is the type of con where volunteers can earn membership next year by working, find out how they are going to track this information. If formal signatures are required, more than just the Masquerade Director must be able to sign work cards. The people should also include the Back Stage Manager, House Manager and Head Check-in. The master check-in sheets can be used as a cross reference, if required.

Backstage Announcements Checklist

Announcements for backstage briefing to contestants and den people. [ ] items may or may not need to be announced or are choices. Check them off when you prepare this sheet

BRIEF DEN LEADERS AND DEN HELPERS
BEFORE CONTESTANTS CHECK -IN STARTS
& ANNOUNCE TO CONTESTANTS ONE HOUR BEFORE AND AGAIN
ONE HALF HOUR BEFORE

- No smoking backstage!
- If you have not checked in yet and received your 3x5 card with your entry number on it, please come to the check-in table at _____
- No unauthorized personnel allowed backstage!
- All roadies must have security badges - see check-in. All unbadged personnel will be ejected.
- The masquerade starts officially at _____
    - [ ] You will be given a 15 minute warning and a five minute notice.
- Stage entrances are: _____
- Stage exits are: _____
- Reminder: we will have catchers to help you on and off the stage. Please let them assist you. If you have special problem entering or exiting, tell the Backstage Manager so we can be prepared
    - [ ] areas to be careful of?
    - [ ] stair/height problems?
    - [ ] stage floor problems?
- After exiting, contestants go where?
    - [ ] there is contestant seating (where)
    - [ ] there is no contestant seating in the audience. Please return to the green room.
- Last minute stage walk-through will be allowed for...
    - [ ] all
    - [ ] weapons/presentation check
    - [ ] those with large groups or special problems
    - [ ] only by special arrangement
    - [ ] approximate time walk-though will start: _____
- The repair table is located _____ and we can assist you with emergency repairs there. In addition, we also have:
    - [ ] full length mirror
    - [ ] ironing board and iron
    - [ ] steamer
    - [ ] sewing machine
    - [ ] screened dressing area
- You can find water and munchies _____. Ask your Den Leaders to help you get these.
- Nearest bathroom to be used by the contestants is located _____
- [ ] The Workmanship Judges will be arriving at _____
    - [ ] The judges are _____who will be located _____
    - [ ] Workmanship judging is optional, but we encourage you to see the judges - who knows, you might win something!.
    - [ ] Workmanship judging will end at _____
    - [ ] with no final call
    - [ ] with a final call
- The MC is _____

- The MC
    - [ ] will be available to review presentations at _____
    - [ ] will not be available
    - [ ] will only review upon request
- [ ] Weapons check is required for all contestants carrying anything remotely resembling a weapon.
    - [ ] Anyone drawing weapons must have their presentation checked ahead of show time.
    - [ ] All live steel pieces not being drawn must be peace bonded.
    - [ ] Weapons check will begin at _____ by _____
- Photos will be taken for:
    - [ ] official con (where) _____
    - [ ] fan photo (where) _____
    - [ ] Official photos
        - [ ] will be available for viewing: _____
        - [ ] will not be available
        - [ ] maybe purchased from _____
- [ ] Judging photos for the judges will be taken at _____
    - [ ] Please be sure your costume has been photographed before the masquerade starts. Den Leaders please keep track of your den's status.
- After the masquerade is over, award certificates can be picked up at _____
- Documentation and media can be picked up at _____
- [ ] Judging photos
    - [ ] will be returned. Pick-up: _____
    - [ ] will not be returned.
- [ ] This masquerade is being recorded.
    - [ ] After the masquerade the video will be shown at _____
    - [ ] The masquerade video may be purchased. See: _____
- If you forget any of this or need any special help, ask your Den Leaders. That's what we're here for! Good luck!

Fifteen Minute Warning Announcement
- Attention, please. It is fifteen minutes to show time. We will begin lining up shortly, so please get ready.
- [ ] If you have not yet seen the Workmanship judge and want to do so, please go now.
- [ ] If you have not yet had your judging photo taken, do so now.
- Den Leaders, please begin assembling your dens in numerical order.

Five Minute Warning
- It is now five minutes to show time. You should be lined up in order by den. Den Leaders, please check your den. Den Helpers, please assist.
- Reminder, all contestants -you will be exiting _____ and going to:
    - [ ] fan photo located _____
    - [ ] contestant seating located _____
    - [ ] returning back here to the green room
- Don't forget to let the catchers help you off stage. That's what they're there for. And stick around for the awards - you never know, the judges may love you!
- Good luck to you all!

Judges
&
Judging

-- Section 8 --

Selecting good judges is a make-or-break feature of the masquerade, and not only for the contestants. The audience will react very vocally if they think the judging is poor! Also, if contestants feel they will be judged by good judges, they will be more apt to compete and give you a good show. If they think they will be judged by the guy who only likes scantily-clad ladies, the artist who draws only spaceships, and a tipsy Guest of Honor, they won't. So great care should be taken in selecting judges.

What Makes a Good Judge?

1. Some knowledge of the costume art

This doesn't mean every judge needs to be an active costumer. Artists who have drawn good costume art, photographers who have seen and photographed a lot of costumes, people with some stage or presentation background - all of these have served honorably in the past. But they are being asked to judge costumes, and should know something about what it takes to design, make and wear them.

2. Takes judging seriously

A good judge considers it an honor to be asked to judge and is conscientious in the performance of their duties. They arrive sober, pay attention, score carefully, do not make jokes during the presentations, and try to do the best and fairest job they can.

3. Free from obvious bias

Many people will openly declare a bias against certain types of costume - elven ladies, ugly monsters, heavy glitz, silly shtick etc. If someone openly tells you or others that they don't think certain kinds of costumes should get prizes, they probably shouldn't be asked to judge.

4. Reasonable objectivity

It is impossible to divorce oneself completely from knowledge of the people on stage, other competitions, similar costumes etc., especially if one has been judging a lot. But you should try to recruit judges who will make an honest effort to see each costume as new and each costumer as a total stranger on stage. Some folks simply can't put their personal feelings aside, and again, these folks shouldn't be asked to try.

5. Ability to make up their mind

Some folks simply dither or are afraid of offending others. They score everyone the same, and can't come to a decision. This can make the judging deliberations take forever. A good judge is not afraid of their own opinions, to give both low and high scores, and to explain why to fellow judges.

6. Willingness to see different points of view

While judges must have the courage of their convictions, they must also be willing to listen to those of the other judges, and compromise to reach the best collective decision. Different judges will be impressed by different strengths and weaknesses and all points of view should be considered.

Assembling a panel of judges

A panel of judges should be balanced among many areas of expertise. You will want to have at least one experienced judge who knows the ropes administratively and can keep things moving in the deliberation room. You will want knowledge of design, construction, and presentation on your panel. You will want at least one judge who is familiar with recreation and media sources such as comic books, movies and tv shows. You might balance your panel by gender, levels of costuming experience, or even geography.

Check out your potential candidates discreetly before asking them to see if they meet the criteria above. Be especially aware of personality mix, since some folks simply can't judge with each other. When you invite each candidate, tell them who the other judges will be. Confirm with each that they can judge with the others.

The GOH challenge

It is quite common for the convention committee to ask you to let the Guest of Honor or other convention dignitary be a judge. Some of these folk are knowledgeable, dedicated judges and are a welcome addition. Some aren't.

First try to find out which you are dealing with. Your Concom will probably know the type of personality they have invited. If you get one who isn't knowledgeable or who has a difficult personality, you may graciously give them the privilege of selecting one costume as the GOH's Choice, and personally awarding that entry their prize. This flatters them while isolating them from the rest of the judging panel. You may also discuss the problem candidly with your Senior Judge. They may tell you that they can handle the person in the deliberations. In any event, it is the Masquerade Director's responsibility to provide good judges and you will have to work with them or around them.

Briefing the judges

This is an often-forgotten, but essential step.

Before the convention, confirm your judges in writing. Provide each with a copy of the rules and ask that they read them before they come. Note any special prizes they may be asked to give, since many conventions have traditional awards, a judge may not know about. Ask them to come in costume if they can, (this is called "Putting Your Credentials on Your Back") or formal evening attire. Tell them when and where they are to meet. Ask them to prepare a short introduction for themselves to be read by the MC and to bring it. Ask them to stop by registration and let you know they have arrived.

If your budget allows, have the judges taken to dinner ---EARLY. This makes sure that 1) your judges are in a well-fed good mood 2) they don't drink too much 3) they arrive in good time and all together.

At the judges' call, show them where they will sit. Explain the judging forms and how they will score. Remind them of any special quirks in the rules and awards. Introduce them to their clerk. Tell them their clerk will take them to the deliberation room during the judging intermission. Collect their introductions to give to the MC. Have them sign the award certificates while they are waiting for things to begin.

Just before the doors open for general seating, line them up in the order they will be introduced right by the main side entrance

As each is introduced, let him/her go on stage so the audience can see them, then proceed to their assigned seat at the judges' table. After they have deliberated, find out who is going to announce the awards. Sometimes the MC does, and sometimes the judges like to do it themselves. In any event, let the MC know. After the awards are presented, remember to thank the judges both publicly and individually in person. Invite them to come to the post-mortem if they can, and tell them when and where.

The Workmanship Judges

It is increasingly common for masquerades to give separate awards for workmanship. This is judged backstage before the presentations by a judge or judges especially qualified in the technical skills of costuming. Being judged for workmanship is usually optional on the part of the costumer and should not affect in any way the outcome of the presentation judging from the stage. However, it is a good way to recognize those costumers who do choose to expend the extra effort in crafting their costumes.

If there is to be workmanship judging, judges will also have to be selected with great care and should be people who are recognized by many costumers as knowledgeable in a wide range of areas. The workmanship judges are often asked to judge work in such areas as beading, embroidery, leatherwork, metal work, featherwork, plastics, makeup, as well as normal sewing skills, to name just a few. While no one can be expert in all of these, a reasonable exposure to a fair number of them is desirable. Since there is sometimes only one judge, it is extremely important that they be free of obvious bias and capable of objectivity. In some competitions, presentation judges who are skilled costumers may also judge workmanship.

The workmanship judges are usually requested to come backstage about an hour before the event is due to start. They should be given a quiet corner with a good strong light - a swing arm clamp light on a table is a good solution. A sign should be prominently posted near the judging table "**Workmanship Judging Here.**" The judges will need pens, clip boards with a stack of workmanship judging forms attached.

Since this form of judging is optional, Den Leaders should be advised to encourage those contestants with good work to go and see the judges. The Backstage Manager should warn contestants 15 minutes before start time to see the judges if they have not already done so and wish to be judged. Five minutes before the show starts, the Workmanship Judges are escorted to line up with the rest of the judges for introduction to the audience. Those not seeing the judges before this are out of luck.

The Workmanship Judges views the show from the judging table, so they can see how the workmanship holds up on stage. they will join the other judges in the deliberation room, but will determine the awards in workmanship without their input. Likewise, they will not take part in the deliberations for the presentation awards, but may, upon request, advise the other judges if a particular costume is getting a workmanship award. The judges' clerk will make two copies of the workmanship awards list for the MC and Masquerade Director. Don't forget to have the Workmanship Judges sign the award certificates!

Workmanship awards are usually announced before the presentation awards. Generally, the Workmanship awards, like the presentation awards, are read Novice, Journeyman, Master, Best in Show and are announced from lowest to highest award in each category.

The Workmanship Judges should also be publicly thanked and invited to the post-mortem.

At the Judges' Table: At each judge's position & at yours: (usually 3 regular, 1 workmanship):
- Working pen (check them)
- Glass of water and an extra pitcher of water for everyone
- Pad of paper, or at least some paper; copy of the running order; flashlights.
- Judging forms, in order, with judging photo attached
- Place forms at first judge's position at the end opposite you
- All recreation or other documentation, in numerical order at your place, pack of sticky notes for you
- Calculator for you
- Award certificates to be signed
- Small dishes of hard candy or other munchies make for happy judges

In the Judging Deliberation Room:
- Paper index cards
- Table with enough chairs for all participants; list of running order
- Masquerade rules, pens
- Water or soft drinks
- List of suggested Award Titles
- Bring from judging table the calculator, forms, judging photos, documentation, and certificates

Your main objective is to be the Judges' Assistant. Any other duties you are asked to help with are secondary. It is OK to come in a modest costume as long as your movements are not restricted and no hat or headdress restricts the sight lines of people behind you.

Arrive a little early to get your supplies and a briefing from the Masquerade Director. Find out where the judges' deliberation room is and how to get there quickly. Also note the location of the nearest bathroom, since at least one judge inevitably needs to know. Get the deliberation room set up and ready for your judges. Go back to the ballroom and set up your Judging Table. Get the judging forms from the Masquerade Director and make sure that they are in the running order. Any photocopied documentation should be labeled with the group number. Other documentation should be labeled with a sticky note and their number. The forms should have sticky notes stating that there is documentation. Put the documentation in numerical order so it will be easy for you to find and pass to the judges as needed.

Make sure you have all judging photos a half hour before the start (hopefully). These should be stapled to the top of the forms or in a neat stack in numerical order. If any are missing, have a Den Helper tell the Backstage Manager who you are missing.

Once the judges show up in the ballroom, ask them to start signing the award certificates. Show them where each will be seated, and take charge of any personal belongings they don't want to take onstage during their introductions. If no one comes for them, take them to the main side entrance five minutes before the start time and ask them to wait in the wings. At this time, go find out from the Backstage Manager or Masquerade Director if there have been any changes to the running order. Go back to your place and make any necessary changes to the stacks.

The stack of forms should be in front of the first judge. You will sit after the last judge. After each judge sees the form, they will pass it down so it ends up in front of you. If they are scoring on the form, add up the score and circle it.

At the end of the presentations, gather up all the forms, documentation and supplies. Lead the judges to the Judging Room. Once there, sort all forms by division and if the judging photos are in a stack, sort them by division as well. Make sure each set of documentation is reunited with its form. If the scores are on the form, order the forms with highest scores on top, lowest on the bottom.

The judges may request that you also separate out originals from recreations. (If the judges want things another way, do it however they request.)

Note all awards on the judging form and on index cards (one per award) with the award name, division, costume title and contestant's name. Write clearly. (THIS IS KEY!) After the judges have determined the final order of the awards, write down 2 clean legible copies of the awards in the order they are to be read on standard sheets of paper. Give the index cards and the paper lists to the Masquerade Director only! Take all of the forms, notes, documentation and judging photos out of the Judging Room. Leave no written notes behind in wastebaskets!

After the masquerade is over, separate the documentation and judging photos from the judging forms. The Masquerade Director gets the forms and any notes by the judges immediately. No one else is allowed to see these. The judging photos and documentation go to the Backstage Manager to distribute or to the Masquerade Director, however you have been instructed. If the judges have no more need of your services, you are done after you return your supplies to the Masquerade Director.

If anyone asks you about anything that went on during the judging, remind them you are not allowed to say anything about it. *Confidentiality must be maintained.* However, remind them that they may ask the judges directly for each one's opinion.

JUDGING THE SCIENCE FICTION & FANTASY MASQUERADE
- A PERSONAL VIEW BY ONE WHO'S DONE IT

by Janet Wilson Anderson

This article is revised from one written originally for CostumAPA. I have received many requests to turn that into a how-to article and this is it. Why am I the one sounding off on this subject? Because 1) I'm qualified: I've been a judge at Worldcons three times now, plus I've judged a number of regional and local conventions as well. And 2) I'm not afraid to tell it as I see it! So herewith are my views on the subject. NOTE: The opinions expressed below are my personal opinions and do not represent any other group/person.

Part I – Criteria for Judging a Costume

WHAT DO YOU LOOK FOR WHEN YOU JUDGE.A COSTUME?: This is the question I get asked most often as a judge. So here are my criteria. Other judges may put their priorities in a different order, but this is a good place for the first-time judge to start.

I. Costumes First!

First of all, I look at the costumes. Presentation is important, but for me, particularly when judging Novices and Journeymen, a good costume will overcome a so-so presentation and get an award. If two entries are tied for the top prize, I will personally opt for the one with the more challenging costumes. After all, this isn't an acting or stagecraft competition; it's a costume competition. So what do I look for in a costume?

A. Originality: I evaluate costumes on originality first. While I try to clear my mind of everything I've ever seen before and look at each competition with fresh eyes, costumes that try something I've not seen before will still impress me more. This is particularly true the further up in the skill divisions you go. I expect more originality from Master division entries, because their skills permit it. Of course, this isn't the first criterion for Recreation costumes, but even then there can be originality in the choice of costume recreated.

B. Execution of Design: I evaluate costumes on execution of the design concept. Is it cleanly done? Are there extraneous bits distracting my eye - too much glitz in the wrong place, for example. Does the workmanship visible from the stage look neat? (I mark costumes down that are falling apart before my eyes, or which are obviously missing the finishing details they need.) Is the choice of colors appropriate? This has caused a number of lost points over the years - colors that clash, or main characters overshadowed by a minor character in bright red. Color happens to be part of my main career and I'm particularly pleased when I see it well used.

C. Unity of Concept: In a group I look for unity of design concept. Do all the members of the group look like they belong together, whether from the same universe, culture or story? This is probably this single biggest error made by groups - no unity of design. I know it's fun to have everyone doing their own thing. But if three of the group are in sexy-lady outfits and the others are swathed to the ears, it's apt to look strange, especially if two are in purple, one green, one yellow, and one black. (Yes, I'm describing a real group here. I might note they were supposed to be the same entity.) Wilson Anderson's Rule: a group shall look like it didn't just happen to meet accidentally.

D. Consistency of Execution: Again, in a group, consistency of execution is important. If one costume is really poorly done, it will drag down the cumulative effect of the group. If you have one spectacularly done costume, it should be given prominence and not overshadow the main character in the group. Off-balanced execution is the second biggest problem I've seen with groups. Bjo Trimble said it years ago: A group is only as good as its weakest member.

II Workmanship

If workmanship is being judged, I focus on the costume itself, and not on the costumer wearing it. I look at everything up close to see that the costumer has executed their concept and design with skill, and used appropriate construction techniques. I also look at any documentation to see how well the workmanship matches the original concept and design.

A contestant presents their costume to the judges, either in the Green Room before the masquerade or in a separate judging session.

Time is Limited. I have a fixed time for each costume based on the total time available and the number of entries. When the time is up, I need to move to the next entry to make sure everyone has their slot. For large groups, I may allow multiple time slots, depending on the size of the group.

Plan Ahead. Think about how you want to present your costume ahead of time. Some judges want the costumer to take the lead, especially for experienced costumers, while others will ask questions, especially for newer costumers.

Tell Me What's Right – Not What's Wrong. Tell me about what aspects you are the most proud of or that I should give special attention to. Never tell me what is wrong! If it's obvious you won't have to tell me and if I don't notice, why point it out?

III. Presentation

After looking at the costume elements of design and execution, I weigh the presentation. For me, the purpose of presentation is to increase the impact of the costume. I've seen a number of presentations actively hurt the judges' ability to evaluate the costume. Artsy lighting so dim the costume can't be seen. Staging that keeps the most impactful member of a group clear in the back. Blocking that obscures key elements of the costume.

As a judge this drives me crazy! I want to see the costumes, and if you want an award from me, you should let me see your work at its best advantage. Unless we are dealing with the category of Humorous Schtick where costume is not really the point and presentation (especially timing!) is every-thing.

Show the Costume to its Best Advantage: I look for a presentation that shows off the costume to its best advantage. I love a presentation that has no wasted moves, where every element displays some new aspect of the costume for my view. I know that you sometimes need a little time and stage movement to establish character, but far too much time is spent on this in most presentations.

Don't Bore Me! This is a visual art, and I use a rule of thumb that says something new should come into view about every 10-15 seconds on stage. This could be a costume mutation, a new prop, a new member of a group. Just to stand on stage and wave your arms for 60 seconds, or for a group to parade on stage and stand there flapping their capes for 3 minutes is really boring.

Let Me See You! likewise, to scuttle across stage at the speed of light doesn't do much good either. Or to design a costume with a beautiful back and let the judges see it for a microsecond as you whirl around.

Of course. a good presentation adds immeasurably to a good costume. And at the more skilled levels and for Best in Class/Show, both count. But a bad costume will lose more points with me than a bad presentation.

Past History Shouldn't Count: I've changed my mind about one element of judging over the years. I used to feel that, as an experienced costumer, it was part of my judging qualifications to be able to take into consideration the previous costumes done by a particular costumer or costumes throughout history. To say, particularly in the Master's division, "This isn't up to 'X's best work, and so should be scored less than 'Y', who has really come a long way." Or to be able to say "I've seen 432 Snow Queens and this one doesn't stack up to the one Jacqui Ward did at Chicon." I no longer think this is appropriate.

See Each Costume for the First Time: I feel it is a judge's obligation to look at each costume and at each competition as if she/he had never seen any other of the contestant's work or similar costumes before. I am now approaching each masquerade with a costume standard against which I measure each entry (see above for the composition of that standard), but to the extent humanly possible, I clear my mind of knowledge of specific costumes seen before. As a judge, I don't personally know a soul on that stage. This also eliminates the problem associated with entering the same costume in different masquerades. As far as I'm concerned, I'm seeing each costume for the first time, and judging it only in the context of the masquerade in which it is entered.

An Absolute Standard: So, my standard is now an absolute one, and varies only by the level of the masquerade. I do judge more stiffly at a Worldcon and Costume-Con than I do at a Westercon or a Baycon. But everyone is judged the same, without regard to their personal history or previous masquerades.

Personal Bias: If the above is the policy for all judges, then the question of judges judging Significant Others also goes away. As a judge you know no one on stage personally. In the real world, though, it can be a perceptual problem for the audience and for those contestants unwilling to admit their own shortcomings. (It's much easier to blame bias than one's own failings.) So as a judge, I abstain from scoring any member of my family or entering into the deliberations about their entry, and insist that if any of them wins an award, my abstention be so announced. I think it is appropriate action for judges in general.

Real Bias: Fact is, every single judge that ever judged is biased in some way. Judge 'X' likes glitz; judge 'Y' hates ugly monsters; judge 'Z' thinks techy props are neat. That's why we have a panel of judges, not just one. But to the extent that judges can put personalities aside and just look at the costumes, judging can be as fair as possible. And for those who can't, we quickly learn who they are and try to avoid using them as judges again.

Sandbagging: Is it the judges' obligation to take action against sandbaggers (those who compete in a division below their skill level or who compete a costume that has won previously in a more challenging competition)? In an absolute sense, I think the answer is no.

It is the Masquerade Director's job to see that the entrants abide by them. The more knowledgeable the Director, the easier to spot people competing in inappropriate classes or costumes beyond the normal range and steer them into higher divisions.

The judges should judge what they are given to judge. If someone is entered in

Novice and the Director has let them so enter, they will be judged against the Novice class entrants. To penalize an entrant for something the Director has sanctioned is not a judge's task. And it really confuses the audience if someone in an outstanding costume is overlooked in the judging or given a prize in a higher division than they competed in. Now in the Real World, things are sometimes a little less clear.

The Masquerade Director Sets the Rules, Not the Judges: As a judge, it is my obligation to be familiar with the rules of the competition I'm judging. A copy of those rules should be in the judges' room during their deliberation, and should be given to them prior to the start of the judging by the Director during the judges' briefing.

This isn't always the case, so the judges should have the right to ask the Director for clarification of a contestant's standing. If the judges know something the Director doesn't, they better let them know. It then is up to the Director to rule on whether the contestant gets bumped up in Class or stays as entered.

In any event, it is the Director's call, in my opinion. (It would be nice if the Director let the contestant know too.} This also goes for things like costumes that took prizes in more demanding masquerades and are now "competing down". As a judge, I've never seen this costume before officially. Obviously, the more experienced the Masquerade Director, the less likely sandbagging should be.

Part II: Judging Procedures

Forms: The pass-along form used by many masquerades can work, but I've heard a lot of comment that it's hard not to be influenced by what the previous judges have scored. I prefer a method that lets each judge operate independently, either by individual score cards or a fold-up-from-the-bottom-as-you-score sheet that hides each judges' score from the others. This also eliminates the problem of the last judge in line unduly influencing the total score. (I'm not saying it's happened, but on a straight-score basis, it could).

Scoring: Scoring should be a guide to the judges' deliberations, not the final determination. *I hate straight score judging!!* No matter what score I give to an individual entry at the time, I reserve the right to change my mind after I've seen the entire show. A judging system that just adds up the scores and declares first, second, third on that basis is the pits and unfair to costumes later in the show. I strongly feel that scores should only be a guide to the final awards.

Scoring Scale: There's been a lot of debate on 10 point systems, versus 5 point systems. I personally use a 10 point system, but if I'm judging with people who prefer 5, I simply use half points: 7 points on a 10 scale= 3 1/2 points on a five scale. Since it should only be a guide, it's not worth getting steamed up over. Use what's comfortable to allow you to make discriminations among the contestants.

Actually Making the Award Determination - Two Judging Procedures to Use:

I. If you have a pass-along form and a judges' clerk to add up scores. use this:

A. Have the clerk add up the total score for each entry as the masquerade progresses.

B. The clerk sorts the scores into piles by division, highest score on top.

C. The judges look first at all the highest scores without regard to division to see if they can reach a consensus on Best in Show. There may be a strong difference of opinion, which can be resolved by giving two Bests (if they happen to be for two totally different types of costumes, e.g. Recreation and Original or Solo and Group, etc.) Or by waiting until all the potential candidates have been discussed. Or by reaching a consensus that no Best in Show award should be given.

D. The pile for each division is then evaluated. There is often a natural break in the scores with those above notably more impressive than those below. This makes it easy to tell the potential award winners. In any case, the entire pile should at least be discussed on a yes/no basis, to allow for any changes of heart a judge may have had after seeing the entire show.

E. The judges then discuss each entrant that any one of them feels should be considered for an award. Again, they may choose to start by determining Best in Class or wait till all candidates have been discussed.

F. As an award winner is identified, an award name may be determined at that time. If the panel is stumped over an appropriate name, it is best to go on and come back to the problem name after all the others are decided.

G. The same procedure is followed for all skill divisions used.

H. After all the awards are determined, the order the awards should be read in is decided. Traditionally, the order is Junior, Novice, Journeyman, Master, Best in Show. Within each division, the lowest award is read first, leading up to Best in Class. Also, by tradition, Judges' Choice

II. If each judge is scoring independently, the procedure is similar except in its initial stages.

A. The judges refer to their own notes for the initial discussion on Best in Show. It is each judge's responsibility to identify the likely candidates for this honor as she/he views the show.

B. After this award has been given, the judges' clerk divides all the entry forms into division and sorts them by entry number so the judges can identify them in their notes.

C. The judges take each division's pile and sort the entries one by one, using a "Definitely yes/ Maybe/ No Award" decision. This should be done very fast, with each judge referring to their own notes for the sort. If any one judge feels strongly about an entry but others disagree, put it in the "Maybe" pile for further consideration. This saves time and argument!

D. They then go through the "Definitely Yes" pile to find consensus on the Best in Class candidates. After that is determined, they go through the rest of the "yes" group, assigning award names.

E. Then the judges take a look through the "maybe's" to see if any of them, after consideration, should receive an award as well. Often, these will be candidates for Honorable Mention or Honored for Excellence.

F. And lastly, if time permits after all the divisions are sorted and awards named, a last look through the "no's" for anything worth reconsidering is a fair thing to do.

G. After all the awards are determined, they are saved and recorded as above.

H. It is particularly important in this system that each judge destroy their own notes!

Either of these two procedures is reasonably quick, allows for consideration of each entry in comparison with the entire show, and ensures each entry receives a fair hearing.

Recommendation on Forms and Procedures: I would prefer a judges' contestant list for each judge with room on the page to score individually. I prefer the independence of separate scoring because it allows each judge to use whatever system suits him/her. It frees the judges' clerk from a lot of arithmetic. And there are not tell-tale total scores anywhere to cause flack if they are found. ("I scored higher than X, but she got an award and I didn't" has been heard!)

There would still be a form for the judges to see that would include the relevant information the contestant wants the judges to know and with attached documentation. This form would be passed along during the presentation and would be available in the judges' room.

Judging Photos - A Must! Every entry should have a judging photo if at all possible. The judges' clerk would put the photos in order by entry number, so the judges can refer to them to refresh their memory. If there are more than 20 entries this is the best way to be sure no one disappears from memory.

Part III: Awards and Titles

The most common mistake made by inexperienced Concoms and Masquerade Directors is to think that limiting the number of awards and/or pre-determining the titles/categories of awards will shorten the judging time. This is totally false. Telling the judges what awards to give just makes the job harder, as you try to force a wide mix of costumes into a pre-set list of titles.

{As a bit of a maverick, I have been on a judging panel where we just taped over the trophy title and gave the costume the award title it deserved - which wasn't what the director had had pre-engraved.}

I prefer to have the freedom to award whatever titles are appropriate to the costume. It is a judging panel's obligation to take a great deal of care in selecting titles.

THE OVERRIDING PRINCIPAL FOR AWARD TITLES: Make the awardee feel good about getting it!

Some guidelines for award titles that I use:

1. MOST and BEST are more satisfying to win than SECOND or THIRD, I'd rather personally be the best at anything than only second, or even worse, third. We're all in this for egoboo, so why not maximize it? MOST or BEST also tells the audience just what the judges thought was worthy of an award.

2. **HONORED FOR EXCELLENCE** is more satisfying to win than HONORABLE MENTION. If a costume entry in its totality isn't up to a Most or Best, why not recognize the element of the entry that the judges did think worthy? If the costume had excellent use of color, or spectacular wings, why not give an award for excellence for those things, instead of the "not quite good enough" award of Honorable Mention? As a contestant wouldn't you rather be recognized for what you did right?

3. Silly titles belong only to costumes that are trying to be humorous. It is quite disheartening to get a frivolous award for a costume you worked your buns off for. On the other hand, if you are trying to amuse the audience and succeed, the judges should have the license to award you something like "Too Cute to Live", or "Best Rockumentation".

4. If a category is announced ahead of time (e.g. Time-travelers, Star Trek, etc.) the judges should make every effort to award a prize for that category. If absolutely nothing comes up to snuff, then the MC should announce that the judges gave no award in category "X". This clues both contestants and audience. Of course, it's still better if you don't have to deal with pre-set categories at all!

5. Embarrassing titles should be avoided. Would you like to tell your mother/co-workers that you won Best Turd when you were going for Best Earth Mother? Titles like Most Graphic, Most Pornographic, Worst Presentation are not fun to win unless you've made it clear that's what you were going for. Of course, there are exceptions, but I really don't feel any serious costume deserves a frivolous or embarrassing title.

6. There can/should be more than one award given for Recreation costumes. if more than one deserves it. If Recreation is judged on the skill level system, not as a separate absolute category, then it, too should have a full range of awards available. Some ideas that come to mind: Best Characterization, Most Authentic, Best Translation from 2-D, Best Japanamation, Honored for Excellence in Accessories, in Attention to Details, etc.

7. Judges' Choice is a title that I regard as second only to Best in Class/Show. This title is useful when everything is so good you don't want to single out just one element as a Most or Best. It is also useful for honoring

entries that have merit not obvious to the casual audience, but noticed by the judges.

I attach a list of titles (expanded from one Marjii Ellers did some years back) that might be of use to future judges. Feel free to copy it, and take it with you when you judge. Having a list of suggested titles has shortened many a judging session for me! Additions also welcome!

BEST IN SHOW - A Personal View: For my money, there is always a Best in Show. I believe it is a judge's obligation to make the fine discriminations necessary to pick a personal Best and a judging panel's obligation to evaluate those discriminations until a resolution is reached. Nowhere is it written that the judges have to agree unanimously. We usually have an uneven number of judges so that ties don't occur. Majority opinion is sufficient to decide.

If the judges are willing to pick enough nits - openly, candidly, and objectively - I believe they can virtually always reach at least majority agreement. If judges do not award a Best in Show, they are tacitly stating that they cannot perform their function of discriminating among diverse costumes/presentations, and it calls into question all other awards they give!

I know this makes a number of people very uncomfortable, especially if there is vehement disagreement among the judges. Here's where the Judges' Choice option comes in, or the option of awarding Best in Show in both Original and Recreation, if that's appropriate. Or if all else fails, 'fess up and award a tie. I think that's less of a cop-out than saying no one was worthy enough to be singled out as Best overall.

HOW MANY PRIZES DO YOU GIVE?: My basic rule is to recognize everything worthy.

In some masquerades this may only be 10%; in others 60%. Usually, in my experience, you run out of "worthy" at about 35 - 40% of entries. I prefer to err on the generous side, since all people are getting out of this is egoboo anyway. As long as what is recognized is genuinely good, what's another piece of paper?

Part IV: Judging Facilities

Judges' Table should be equipped with:

A. Flashlights - judging is very difficult under the best of circumstances. Doing it in the dark is well-nigh impossible! Comcons -

please provide your judges with flashlights or some other lighting source to score by. The little pocket flashlights cost 99 cents each at 7/11 - not a major convention expense.

B. Glasses & water.

C. Pens to write with and spare paper to take notes on.

D. A list of the contestants, costume titles and divisions. (This list can be hand-written right after the masquerade is put in order, [typed is better], and a few copies run off for the crew and the judges.) It helps if this list bears some resemblance to the numbering system used by the MC.

E. A competent judges' clerk to see to our needs and keep the paperwork in order.

Workmanship Judging Area – located in a quiet area of the Green Room or another quiet place were workmanship judging will take place, and equipped with:

A. A table to put ail the papers on.

B. Reasonably comfortable chairs.

C. Pens to write with and spare paper to take notes on.

D. A list of the contestants, costume titles and divisions.

E. A competent judges' clerk to bring us contestants, watch the time, and keep the paperwork in order.

Deliberation Room - a quiet, well-lit place to conduct our deliberations away from the crowd and the costumers and equipped with:

A. A table to put all the papers on.

B. Reasonably comfortable chairs.

C. A near-by bathroom - we will need a comfort stop before starting to judge! It does shorten the judging interval if we don't have to hike miles to the bathrooms.

D. Sodas/other drinkables during the judging are appreciated.

E. A competent judges' clerk to help us stay on track, keep the paperwork in order, and record our decisions.

Part V: Other Responsibilities

Post-Mortem Availability: I do believe it is part of the judges' job to be available, if possible, at the post-mortem. It is not part of the judges' job to defend their decisions. However, procedural explanations may be of assistance to the audience. (Yes, we did see all the recreation documentation: no, the Novice panel did not participate in the Journeyman/Master's judging, etc.)

Private Advice: I also feel it is part of my obligation to offer advice on an individual basis to those costumers who wish to know how to improve for the future. I will point out things that impressed me about winning costumes, and will privately tell someone my own opinion of what could be done better.

Confidentiality: I think it is reprehensible behavior for one judge to tell a contestant that they lost because another judge disliked this or that! That is a violation of the judging confidentiality. You have an obligation to keep the all the proceedings in the judges' deliberations totally private. Remember the old game of gossip? You can imagine what distortions can creep in once the news has passed through a few people. A responsible judge keeps a buttoned lip.

Last Words

As you can see, it isn't easy being a judge. It's a tough demanding job, with few psychic rewards. You can be personally vilified for non-existent bias, considered blind, deaf and stupid, and be called an incompetent fool (or worse). I began judging because I thought it would make me a better costumer to see things from the judge's point of view (and I believe it has).

I continue judging because most folks seem to react favorably when they hear I'm one of those selected to evaluate their work. As long as the costume community thinks I'm a good judge, feels I'm fair to their work, and I keep getting asked, I'll probably keep doing it. I have enough chutzpah to think "Better me, than some I could mention!"

And I'll keep training up the new folks brave enough to give it a try!

Appendix: A Judge's Bill of Rights and Obligations

Judge's Rights
- Judges should be considered fair, unbiased, and competent until proven otherwise.
- Judges shall have the freedom to award prizes to everything they see worthy of them and not to any unworthy.
- Judges need consider no other points of view but their own in their deliberations.
- Judges should be given the equipment/facilities needed to do their job.
- Judges shall be briefed by the Masquerade Director as to the contest rules.
- Judges shall have access to the Masquerade Director during their deliberations, but that Director shall take no part in them.
- Judges shall use whatever scoring system they mutually agreed upon.
- Judges shall be given a competent clerk who understands confidentiality.
- Judges shall not be forced to reveal any of their deliberations.
- Judges shall not be required to defend their decisions to anyone!

Judge's Obligations
- Judges shall give recognition to all worthy costumes.
- Judges shall be familiar with the rules pertaining to the particular masquerade they are judging.
- Judges shall view each masquerade as if it is their first.
- Judges shall view each contestant as if each were a stranger, and disqualify themselves where this might be questioned.
- Judges shall attempt to leave all other personal biases at home.
- Judges should be as expedient in their deliberations as possible.
- Judges should maintain confidentiality about their deliberations.
- Judges should make their advice available to costumers genuinely wishing to improve for the future.

Janet Wilson Anderson

Best in Class / Show
- Judges' Choice
- Honored for Excellence

Most Outstanding
- Most Impressive
- Best Spectacle
- Best Extravaganza
- Most Splendid
- Most Magnificent
- Most Majestic
- Most Spectacular

Most Beautiful
- Most Elegant
- Most Exquisite
- Most Graceful
- Most Glamorous
- Most Brilliant
- Most Charming
- Most Captivating

Best Fantasy
- Best Mythology / Mythological
- Best Pantheon
- Best Deity
- Most Celestial
- Most Mystical
- Best Wizardry

Best Science Fiction
- Most Literary
- Most Scientific
- Most Avant-garde
- Most Advanced
- Most Futuristic

Best Recreation
- Most Authentic
- Most Accurate
- Best Media
- Best Characterization
- Best Adaptation
- Best Comic Book Character

Best Film / TV Character
- Most Detailed
- Most Thorough

Best Design
- Most Artistic
- Most Refined
- Most Subtle
- Best Concept
- Most Visual
- Best Use of Color
- Best Use of Glitz

Most Original
- Most Creative
- Most Clever
- Most Fanciful
- Most Outrageous
- Most Imaginative
- Most Unusual
- Most Provocative
- Most Exotic

Best Presentation
- Best Performance
- Most Dramatic
- Most Theatrical
- Most Compelling
- Best Makeup
- Best Props

Best Alien
- Best BEM
- Best Feline / Equine / Saurian etc.
- Best Creature
- Best Beast
- Best Monster
- Most Monstrous

Most Horrifying
- Most Terrifying
- Most Grotesque
- Most Evil

- Most Villainous
- Best Villain
- Most Menacing
- Most Ominous
- Most Macabre
- Most Spectral

Most Humorous
- Funniest
- Most Amusing
- Silliest
- Cutest
- Wittiest
- Most Comical
- Best Shtick

Most Sophisticated
- Most Aristocratic
- Most Imperial
- Mist Distinguished
- Most Urbane
- Most Opulent
- Most Sentimental
- Most Romantic

Best Tech
- Best High Tech
- Best Electronic
- Best Mechanical

Best Military
- Best Uniform
- Best Weaponry
- Best Armored
- Best Mercenary

Best Barbarian
- Best Ethnic
- Best Folklore

Most Promising
- Best Junior Costumer

The "Bare-Bones" Show,

Good Ideas That Don't Work

-- Section 9 --

If you expect a small competition, or your contestants are likely to be mostly Novices and Journeymen, you can probably get away with a simpler support structure and less equipment. You will still need careful pre-planning, but without the big costumes, large groups and complicated technical presentations, you can do things somewhat simpler.

You will still need a registration form and information/rules sheet and a place to set up registration. You will need a couple of hours to set up the stage area, tech and chairs, and you should ask contestants to check in at least 45 minutes before start time.

You will need someone in charge of your backstage area where the costumers will be assembling, a check-in person, and at least a couple of people to take care of them as Den Leaders. You will need water and straws, for the health of your costumers. You'd best have at least some safety pins, duct tape and glue backstage for emergency repairs.

You will need pushers to help get people onto whatever stage area you are using, even if it just marked out on the floor. Even the simplest costumes can be difficult to move in, or come with things like trains to be moved out of the way. Likewise. you will need a couple of people as catchers to move people off the stage area.

You will need an emcee with a podium and microphone. You will need some way of masking the contestants from the audience on at least one entrance side. (In a pinch we've even used venue blackboards or strung tablecloths on string as improvised pipe and drape.) Try not to have people enter and exit from the same place.

Your judges will need a table and chairs, and a clerk to help them record their awards. You will probably use a Front of House manager to coordinate traffic, security, set-up and tech. You will need a few folks to handle door security and seating flow.

For tech, at a minimum, you will need one spotlight, and someone to control the house lights. You will need two tape decks or CD players and speakers, plus someone to run the equipment. You will want at least two headsets, one for the person calling the masquerade from backstage and one for the person cuing sound and lights.

You will want to set aside an area with good lighting and a plain background for general photo (or you may have the costumers come back on stage during the judging intermission and let all who wish to photograph them in the spotlight.) You will still need award certificates and someone to calligraph them.

This set-up will handle a simple show, but it is very limited in its capabilities for both the costumer and the audience. We have found that the more capabilities we can offer, the more interesting the costumes that are likely to show up and the better the show for the audience! So, we urge you to try to do as much as you can.

Bare-Bones Masquerade Committee Organization

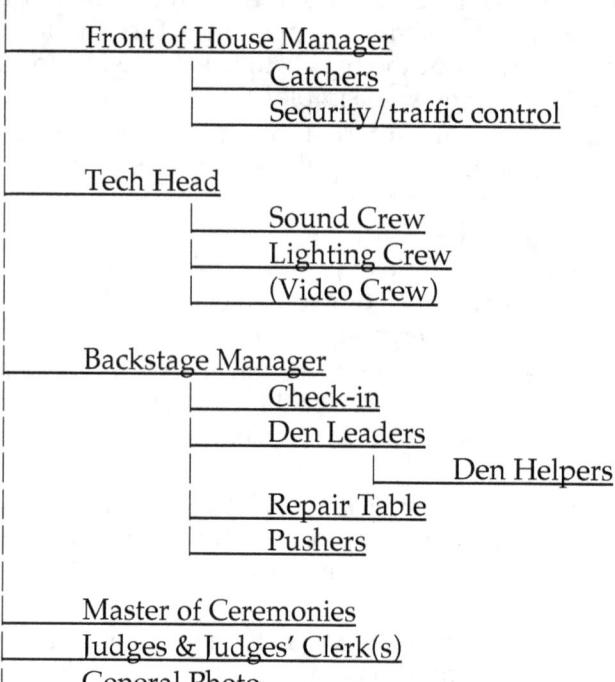

<u>Masquerade Director</u>

    <u>Front of House Manager</u>
        <u>Catchers</u>
        <u>Security/traffic control</u>

    <u>Tech Head</u>
        <u>Sound Crew</u>
        <u>Lighting Crew</u>
        <u>(Video Crew)</u>

    <u>Backstage Manager</u>
        <u>Check-in</u>
        <u>Den Leaders</u>
            <u>Den Helpers</u>
        <u>Repair Table</u>
        <u>Pushers</u>

    <u>Master of Ceremonies</u>
    <u>Judges & Judges' Clerk(s)</u>
    <u>General Photo</u>

This section covers a number of ideas that would seem, on the surface, to be ways of making the masquerade run more smoothly. At various time they have all been tried (some several times!). We list them and their problems, so you can avoid making the same mistakes yourself.

1. Ramps in place of stairs - If your stage is over 1-1/2 feet high, the length of your ramp will be impossibly long when the angle of incline is gentle enough to get tall costumes up it without tilting backwards. A 6 degree ramp (the same decline noted on the highways as "dangerous downhill grade") requires a ramp 19 feet long to rise two feet. Many costumes have strange feet, with hooves, high heels, stilts, or just big bases. These can overbalance dangerously while going up even a gentle ramp. If you have a big, strong pusher crew, they can lift almost anything up onto a stage. (Wheelchairs, robots, BEM's and large props have all been handled in the past!)

2. Giving the judges predetermined award titles - Some conventions think it will shorten the judging time if the judges are given pre-set award titles, such as Best SF, Best Fantasy, Best Media, Most Humorous, Best Trek, etc. The problem arises when either there are no costumes worthy of an award in that specific category, or there is a stunning costume that fits none of the categories assigned. While it is perfectly acceptable and quite common for a masquerade to have a special award or two, perhaps to encourage a certain theme of costume, by requiring the judges to give only predetermined awards, you limit their freedom to recognize all costumes deserving of an award, and may force them to give an award to something otherwise undeserving.

3. Putting the masquerade in order by skill level - With the exception of Junior costumers, who are often grouped together at the beginning of the show so the little kids can get to bed, running the show by class produces a boring show. It may seem fairer to run all the Novices, then all the Journeymen, then all the Masters, but it is actually harder to judge! It is easier for the judges to clear their minds between entries when the difference between entries is greater. And it makes a better show for the audience if there are a lot of mini-climaxes throughout the show, as well as a mix of serious and humorous. In one instance when it was announced beforehand that the show would be run by class, much of the audience didn't even show up for the Novices.

4. Putting the show in order as the entries are turned in - Though less of a problem than running the show by skill level, this leaves your show pacing at the mercy of random chance. You can find yourself with a whole series of costumes on the same theme (three Batmans in a row!) or with all your big technical headaches at the end (since Masters are notorious for waiting till the last minute to get their forms in). It is a bit more trouble to plan the order for your masquerade after all the entries are in, but by so doing, you can control a lot more of the variables, especially tech challenges.

5. Separating "presentations" from "costumes - At one time most presentations were really skits, and most serious costumes were shown fairly simply - almost fashion show style. That day is long gone. Today's costumer plans the presentation as an integral part of the costume itself, and there is no way to separate the two. Limiting the amount of time any given entry can take is a much fairer way of keeping things short.

6. Getting a professional "personality" to emcee the show - MC'ing the masquerade is a difficult skill, unique to this art form. Most professional personalities are unaccustomed to submerging their own personalities to other things happening on stage. Also, many feel that their primary job is to entertain the audience, often at the expense of the costumer trying to perform. We've seen professional entertainers try to "interview" the contestants while they are presenting. We've seen costumers burst into tears after the MC made some supposedly witty crack about their work. And then there's the MC who adlibs instead of following the costumer's text. While there is no question that a certain amount of showmanship is essential to a good emcee, it is better to opt for someone who takes the job seriously and reads clearly, than someone who views it as a chance to boost their own ego.

7. Putting the main spotlight directly in the center back - this may seem the best place for the most direct lighting. However, it is guaranteed to blind the contestants, particularly if you have a center exit. Placement to one side, or even better, use of two side spots will light the costumes better without dangerously affecting the contestant's vision.

[Editor's note: we are actively looking for additions to this article for future editions, so we can avoid re-inventing the square wheel over and over again. Send your contributions to the publisher's address, inside front cover. Credit will be given.]

Forms

-- Section 10 --

PLEASE PRINT VERY CLEARLY!

Entry No. _____

SKILL DIVISION (*check one*): [ ] Novice   [ ] Journeyman   [ ] Master   [ ] Junior (under 13)

CATEGORY FOR JUDGING (check one): [ ] Original design   [ ] Recreation

COSTUME TITLE: _____

COSTUME SOURCE: _____

NAME(S) OF ENTRANTS (*attach second sheet if necessary*) _____

_____

DESIGNED BY _____
(*if different than entrant*)

MADE BY: _____
(if different than entrant)

MAILING ADDRESS FOR COSTUMER / GROUP _____

_____

AUDIO: [ ] Media   [ ] PRINTED TEXT FOR MC TO READ
(*check and attach to this form*)

SPECIAL INSTRUCTIONS FOR MC (*attach second sheet if necessary*) _____

_____

TECH (*check one*): [ ] Default (normal)   [ ] Special Cues (*attach to this form*)

DOMINANT COLOR (*check one*): [ ] Black   [ ] Brown   [ ] Red   [ ] Orange   [ ] Yellow   [ ] Blue
[ ] Green   [ ] Purple   [ ] White   [ ] Gold   [ ] Silver   [ ] Flesh   [ ] Multi-colored

THEME (*check one*): [ ] SF   [ ] Fantasy   [ ] Horror   [ ] Myth   [ ] Beautiful   [ ] Humorous
[ ] Alien   [ ] Movie/TV

Liability Release

I/We have read and understood the rules of this masquerade as set forth in the instructions and agree to abide by them. Further I/We agree to permit photography and/or video-recording, and agree to permit the use and/or dissemination of said photography and/or video recordings. Further, I/We agree to hold the convention, its organizers, and the facility both severally and individually blameless for any accident and/or injury suffered by me/us during the course of this masquerade, except in cases of gross negligence on the part of those cited above

Full legal signature of all entrants. (All entrants must sign. If minor, parent or guardian must sign. *(attach second sheet if necessary)*

_____

_____

_____

_____

_____

_____

(attach second sheet if necessary)

FOR JUDGES USE ONLY
SCORES:

JUDGE 1: _____ JUDGE 2: _____ JUDGE 3: _____ JUDGE 4: _____ TOTAL: _____

(• = normal/default method)

ENTRY # _____

COSTUME TITLE. _____

NAME OF ENTRANTS _____

ENTRANCE: [ ] Main Side*,   [ ] Opposite side   [ ] Both sides

Other (must be approved by Director)_____

_____

EXIT: [ ] Standard*   [ ] Other (must be approved by Director) _____

_____

SOUND:

AUDIO RECORDING: [ ] yes   [ ] no

IF YES, [ ] start after MC introduction*   [ ] or when? (be specific) _____

[ ] stop: after exit*   [ ] or when (be specific) _____

ANY OTHER AUDIO CUES? _____

_____

LIGHTS:

[ ] Full up on entrance, continue throughout presentation?*

[ ] Black out while you get in position on stage, lights up when? _____

_____

FOLLOW SPOTS: [ ] yes*   [ ] no

SPECIAL LIGHTING EFFECTS AND CUES (must be discussed with Lighting head!)

_____

_____

ANYTHING ELSE WE SHOULD KNOW? (*do not surprise your crew!*) _____

_____

Contestants fill out this part.

COSTUME TITLE: _____

CONSTUME WORN BY: _____

MAILING ADDRESS: _____

_____

WORKMANSHIP BY (if different name or multiple names): _____

_____

DO NOT WITE BELOW THIS LINE

Judges' Form

ENTRY # _____

PORTION OF COSTUME [ ] All   [ ] Other (specify) _____

_____

TECHNIQUE(S)
EMPLOYED _____

RELATIVE DIFFICULTY
OF TECHNIQUE(S) _____

EXECUTION: _____

COMMENTS: _____

_____

_____

OVERALL SCORE: _____

NOTES: _____

_____

Divisions: Y=Youth/Junior, N=Novice, J=Journeyman, M=Master

Categories: S=self-made, P=parent-made, O=original, R=recreation

Entry	Division	Categories	Entry title	Entrant name(s)
1.				
2.				
3.				
4.				
5.				
6.				
7.				
8.				
9.				
10.				
11.				
12.				
13.				
14.				
15.				
16.				
17.				
18.				
19.				
20.				

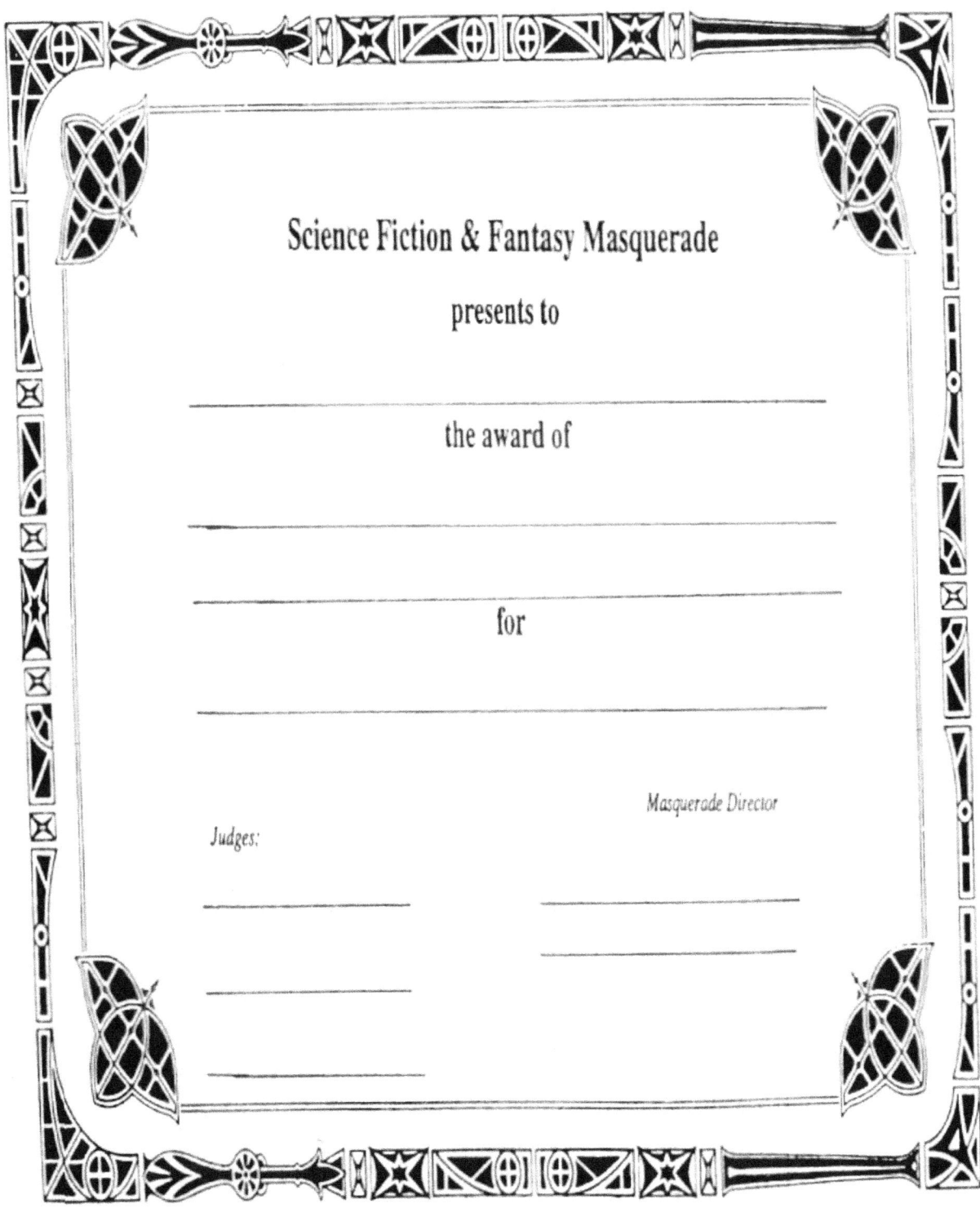

Event: _____

Date: _____

Page _____ of _____

Item	Who brings it	Where during event	Secondary location

Location:_____

Date: _____

Object: _____

Work to be done	Equipment required	Start time	End time	Comments

[ ] Scheduled   [ ] Actual

Location:_____

Date: _____

Object: _____

Name	Job function	Time in	Time out	Comments

Supplies

-- Section 11 --

- Entry forms
- Tech entry forms (if used)
- Rules and information sheets
- Sign-up sheet for reserved seating for available light photography and video
- Sign-up sheet for general photo (if needed)
- Sign-up sheet for volunteers for crew
- Bright 1/2" dots for soundtrack media
- Blank paper
- Pens - lots of pens
- Masking tape
- Pencils
- Magic Markers
- Post-it notes
- Scotch tape
- Scissors
- Stapler, staples, and staple remover
- Large box for completed forms
- Large sign giving registration deadline, call times and location of green room

Repair Kit – see separate list

Munchies and drinkables (enough for both contestants and crew):

- Cups
- Water, water, and more water
- Bendable straws - lots
- Sodas - caffeine and non-caffeine, diet and non-diet, brown, white and orange
- Gatorade, or sugar free lemonade
- Carrot and celery sticks
- Pretzel sticks, other non-greasy but salty finger food
- Wrapped hard candies, like lemon and orange drops - must be non-sticky
- Personal-size packets of M&M's, Gummis
- The keys to munchies selection are:
    - non-greasy, non-sticky
    - bite-size

Check-In Supplies List

- "Check-in Here" sign
- Contestant running order with Den Leader assignments
- Numbered 3x5 cards with Den Leader assignments, blank 3x5 cards
- Post-it Notes, pens
- Blank Paper, Magic Markers, Scotch tape, scissors, stapler
- Crew badges and contestants' gofers badges
- Day-Glo tape in several colors
- List of Den Leaders and Den Helpers
- List of those still needing something - sign release forms, media to be turned in, MC copy to be turned in, etc.

Back-Stage - Other Supplies

- Poster board and Magic Markers pens
- Post-it notes
- Scotch tape, masking tape, stapler
- Blank paper
- Many copies of the running order
- Numbered signs for each den
- "No-Smoking" signs - lots!
- "Contestant and Crew Only" signs for the door
- "Workmanship Judging Here" sign
- "Judging Photos" sign
- "To Stage" sign with arrow

- Tape to mark traffic pattern arrows on the floor to the stage
- Nice to haves: Full Length mirror, pipe and drape or other modesty screening for dressing area, large copy of the Stage Layout map showing traffic flow, photo area, and contestant seating - post near Check-in, iron, ironing board, steamer, coat rack

Judging Photo Area - Supplies

- Clerk to mark pictures and help contestants pose for the camera - preferably two
- If using a Polaroid camera, film - twice as much as you need for one/entry. Marker that writes on Polaroid pictures (Sharpie)
- If using a digital camera, a photo printer, paper and extra toner , and extra memory cards. Marker that writes on printed photos (Sharpie)
- Stapler
- List of running order
- If possible: backdrop - can be section of pipe and drape
- Photo light

Workmanship Judging area - Supplies

- Workmanship judges' forms
- Clip board
- Small table and chair
- Good light - big clamp lights work well
- Pen
- List of running order
- Blank paper for notes

- Glues - White, 527 Craft Cement, Super Glue, 5-Minute Epoxy, Sobo, hot glue sticks, hot glue guns - large and small
- Stapler, staples, staple remover, safety pins (lots)
- Straight pins, bobby pins (lots), hairpins
- Tapes - Masking, Duct, Scotch, Day-Glo for stage marks, electrician's tape, strapping tape
- Spirit gum and spirit gum remover, eyelash cement
- Toupee tape
- Hypoallergenic cold cream and eye makeup remover
- Contact lens / saline solution
- Needles - several sizes, invisible thread, thimble
- Scissors - several pair, tweezers
- Wire - several sizes, wire cutters
- Facial tissues
- Paper towels
- Blank sheets of paper, 3x5 cards
- Post-it Notes
- Pens - lots
- Magic Markers - black and red
- Screwdrivers - regular and Phillips, several sizes, cordless power screwdriver very helpful
- Pliers - several sizes, especially needle nose
- Exacto or craft knife
- Cutting knives
- Crescent wrench
- Hammer

Nice to haves: ironing board, steamer, sewing machine threaded with invisible thread, soldering iron and flux core solder.

Stage Preparation

- Pipe and drape for sides and possibly back of stage, wrenches and screwdrivers to assemble
- Duct tape – a lot, clear Xmas lights for edge of stage, extension cord for Xmas lights
- Day-Glo tape for center stage "X", entrance stairs and exit marks and arrows down exit path

Seating

- Signs for "Photographers", "Handicapped", "VIP", "Contestants" seating; tape, rope, or cord to rope off special seating
- Masking tape to hang signs

Catchers and Walkers

- Small flashlights for exit catchers and aisle walkers
- Running order list for Head Catcher

MC Podium

- MC forms with contestant texts attached
- Running order list
- Water and glass
- Podium light
- Emergency flashlight (full size - pen lights are too small)
- Announcements list
- Before awards are announced, director gets certificates, ribbons and trophies placed on small table near podium

Judges' Table

- Table with chairs for each judge, including workmanship judges, and space on end for judges' clerk
- Water and glasses
- Small flashlights for each judge and clerk
- Pens
- Running order list for each judge and clerk
- Suggested award titles list
- Set of masquerade rules for each judge
- Judging forms
- Contestant judging photo
- Contestants' documentation - attach Post-it Notes with entry number for tracking purposes
- Calculator for clerk
- Award certificates to be signed by each judge before the masquerade starts

Ballroom Check-in

- List of VIP's for special seating
- List of those signed up for available light photo and video

- List of crew heads to direct people to them
- Security badges for front of house crew and catchers, spare flashlight
- Spare copies of running order list
- Pens

Judges' Deliberation Room
- Table with enough chairs for all judges and clerk
- Blank paper
- Running order list
- Masquerade rules
- List of any special awards the judges should give
- Pens
- Water and glasses - sodas are also nice
- From the judges' table, the clerk brings:
    - Judging photos - sorted by division and then entry number
    - Calculator
    - Judges' forms - totaled and sorted by division, then entry number
    - Contestant documentation
    - Suggested award title list
    - Certificates if not yet signed

The following is a recommended minimal equipment list for a midsize masquerade. It will serve as a general guide.

Sound

- 2 tape decks or CD players - good consumer or industrial quality
- 1 power amplifier, 100 watts minimum
- 2 large speakers, 100 watts, PA quality
- 2 microphones, industrial quality
- 1 set headphones
- Lots of RCA interconnect cables for the decks, amp, etc.
- 500 feet or so of speaker wire, heavy duty (#12 or better)
- 1 heavy duty extension cord with power strip
- 2 rolls duct tape

Lights

- 2 light trees, dual crossbar, and sandbags
- 8 to 16 each 6 to 8 inch ellipsoidals, with gels
- 1 dimmer pack
- 1 controller board for dimmer pack 1 follow spot with gels
- 1 208V 3 phase heavy duty extension cord
- 3 standard 115V 3 wire heavy duty extension cords
- 100 feet Cables for the dimmer and controller
- 3 rolls duct tape

Video

- 2 video cameras (If camcorders, VHS)
- 1 tripod
- 1 TV monitor, 25 inch or more
- 500 feet 75 Ohm coax cable, F connectors 2 booster amplifiers, 10dB
- 2 extension cords, 3 wire 50 feet
- 1 extension cord, 3 wire, heavy duty. 100 feet

Headsets - 4 minimum, 9 -10 best!

The above need a common tool kit, with both blade and Phillips screwdrivers, pliers, vise grips, needle-nose pliers, voltmeter, vinyl electrical tape, 5-minute epoxy, F connector crimper, wire cutters, knife, wire stripper, soldering gun and solder, spare F and RCA connectors, some hookup wire, and power phase indicator. It is highly likely these are already in the techs' toolkits that they tend to have with them, but it is a good idea to check.

Registration Signs

- Masquerade registration
    - Open
    - Closed
- Masquerade registration hours
    - Friday: 12:00 to 5:00
    - Saturday: 10:00 to 2:00
- Masquerade takes place in the _____ room _____
- Masquerade starts promptly at _____. Doors open at _____
- Masquerade stage setup starts at _____
- Contestant check-in at _____ in the _____room
    - (post call times of all jobs)
- Photography sign-up here
- Volunteer sign-up here
- Awards and media may be picked up at the post-mortem
    - Room: _____
    - Time: _____
    - Later contact _____ at _____
- Masquerade video will be shown at:
    - Room: _____
    - Time: _____
    - (post copy in green room)

Backstage Signs

- Masquerade contestants and crew, check-in here (post outside the door & an extra to point the way if it's in a comer)
- Photographers, check-in here (near photo area)
- Restricted area - masquerade contestants and staff only
- Check-in
- Workmanship judging
- Judging photos
- Repair kit
- Iron
- Mirror
- Munchies
- Water
- Dressing area
- Den# _____- contestants _____thru _____ (as many as you have dens)
- [Arrow Signs:]
    - To official photo
    - To stage (4 at least)
    - To general photo

Ballroom Signs

- Masquerade seating line starts here
- Line up here for handicapped, VIP seating, and preregistered photo/video
- Doors will open for seating at approximately _____
- Admittance for masquerade crew only
- Ballroom check-in
- Reserved for handicapped seating
- Reserved for VIP seating
- Reserved for available light photo/video
- Reserved for official photo/video

General

- No smoking! (many, posted everywhere)
- No admittance! (posted on all extra doors and judges' room)

Janet Wilson Anderson is known for the style of the costume she creates, her stage presentations, and her impeccable workmanship. Janet was also essential in the formation of the International Costumers' Guild (ICG). She brought her Fortune 500 businesswoman's mentality and expertise to bear on the second chapter of the ICG, Costumer's Guild West, as well as the overall organization's beginnings. Janet has also been a big influence on how Costume-Con fashion shows were and are run, always trying to raise their credibility to the level not only of the competition events, but also of the real world fashion shows that she had so much experience with. Janet received the ICG Lifetime Achievement Award in 1994.

Cat Devereaux was active in costume fandom since the early 1980's. She also created the non-profit Alley Cat Scratch Costumes, one of the largest free informational and costume-supportive websites on the internet. She worked every position in masquerades, and helped organize and run special events backstage, including the Worldcon Hugo Awards. She also did costume design for film, video, and stage. Cat was president of the Costumer's Guild West, Dean of Costume College, and editor of the International Costumers' Guild's *Costumer's Quarterly* magazine. She received the ICG Lifetime Achievement Award in 2005. Cat Devereaux passed away in 2020.

Gary Anderson's costumes were known for great awful puns, long before he entered the fray and got involved in the costuming community. But once in, he never caved, and stayed true to his own sense of humor. His other passion was filk, and he was instrumental in developing modern filk in southern California. He helped to start ConChord, which he worked on and also chaired, and was one of the founding directors and officers of Interfilk, serving as its clerk until his death from cancer in 1998. Gary was married to Janet Wilson Anderson. He received the ICG Lifetime Achievement Award in 1998.

Russell Breighton "Rusty" Dawe is a video game designer, on-line environment designer, programmer, project leader, and manager. In his alternative persona, he is a Reiki master, weatherworker, writer, teacher, and has walked his spiritual path quietly as a solitary practitioner. Rusty was heavily involved in the early years of running the Bay Area Regional Science Fiction and Fantasy Convention (BayCon) in the early 1980's, doing registration and videography.

Richard Foss is a Los Angeles fan who has worked many Loscons and other conventions. He is a member of LASFS and SCIFI, and chaired Loscon 16 in 1990. Along with his brother Wolf Foss, he was Fan Guest of Honor and Toastmaster at Windycon 19 in 1992. Richard is a journalist, author, culinary historian, and a lecturer. He authored 10 science fiction stories that were published in major markets, including *Analog* and in anthologies. He has written for newspapers and magazines for over thirty years, and has written two food-related books. He is the Executive Director of COLLAGE: A Place for Art and Culture, a non-profit educational and arts organization.

Craig Jones has worked as an audio/visual technician for several decades. His theater production credits include Sound Designer, Stage Manager, Audio Technician, and Lighting Technician, and he has been in charge of the audio/visual division of several conventions. In addition, Craig has produced two documentary multi-media shows, has been the editor of two newsletters, and is a published author of non-fiction articles. He has a special interest in the production of costume contests, particularly in the area of sound.